The Scholarship Series in Biology

General Editor: W. H. Dowdeswell

Nature Reserves and Wildlife

THE SCHOLARSHIP SERIES IN BIOLOGY

Nature Reserves and Wildlife

Eric Duffey

Head of Lowland Grassland Research Section,
Monks Wood Experimental Station

Heinemann Educational Books

Heinemann Educational Books Ltd

LONDON EDINBURGH MELBOURNE AUCKLAND TORONTO
HONG KONG SINGAPORE KUALA LUMPUR
NEW DELHI IBADAN NAIROBI JOHANNESBURG
LUSAKA

ISBN 0 435 61256 5
© Eric Duffey 1974
First published 1974

Published by
Heinemann Educational Books Ltd
48 Charles Street, London W1X 8AH

Printed in Great Britain by
The Whitefriars Press Ltd,
London and Tonbridge

Preface

The study of wildlife conservation as a scientific problem is one of the most recent developments in applied ecology, although public concern for the preservation of plants, animals, and landscape has a comparatively long history. It is perhaps too early to claim that conservation ecology has already become a subject in its own right, because so few well-studied examples are available to demonstrate the nature of the problems and how they might be solved. Nevertheless, progress in recent years has been encouraging enough for us to take stock of the achievements to our credit and to examine the trends in current developments.

Although this book is primarily concerned with the scientific aspects of conserving wildlife on nature reserves, the problems discussed have a good deal in common with the care and preservation of almost any type of unspoilt country which provides rural amenities for the public. Such countryside includes many habitats which act as reservoirs for wildlife, particularly ponds, hedgerows, copses, path and roadside verges, railway cuttings, gravel pits, and other types of excavation. If these are to be preserved as valuable components of the landscape—now accepted by an increasing number of people—the same ecological principles must be applied as on land managed as nature reserves.

It is now twenty-six years since the Wildlife Conservation Special Committee reported to Parliament in 1947, and perhaps we should ask whether our objectives are still the same as those defined at that time. In essentials they are. The main purpose of our National Nature Reserve series still is to 'comprise as large a sample as possible of all the many different groups of living organisms, indigenous or established in this country, as part of its natural flora and fauna', and we still acknowledge that the 'management of these areas will entail the most detailed scientific maintenance policy'. But in some ways we have far outstripped the most optimistic recommendations in the 1947 White Paper[1] : the seventy-three proposed National Nature Reserves (England and Wales), covering about 70 000 acres (29 165 ha), had by 1973 become 135 sites with a total acreage of 278 537 (116 057 ha) (including Scotland). The Sites of Special Scientific Interest now number 3165 (over two million acres: over 833 000 ha) and there has been a tremendous growth in the activity of the voluntary conservation movement through the County Naturalists' Trusts. By the end of 1972 the Trusts had established 700 reserves covering over 43 000 acres (17 916 ha), a development quite unforeseen by the pioneers of the 1940s.

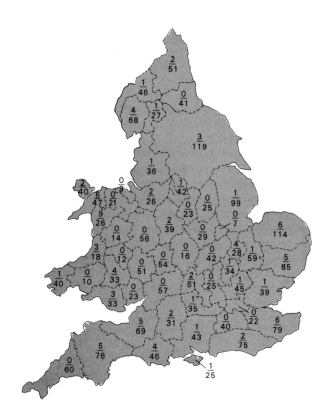

Figure 1. Number of National Nature Reserves (numeral above line) and Sites of Special Scientific Interest (below line), per county, in England and Wales (compiled by John Sheail).

As the conservation movement gathered momentum in the years following 1947, it generated great enthusiasm for its cause among many sections of the public, both professional and amateur. We are still on the crest of this wave, but how far are we succeeding in striking our roots deep enough to maintain the cause in the future? And are we sufficiently flexible in our thinking to adapt our research to the new demands which will surely be made on our nature reserves and open spaces in the future as a result of population increase, more leisure time, and changing educational requirements? Although the needs of wildlife must always be the first objective of our nature reserves, there is little doubt that many will have to absorb additional demands in the years to come, particularly increased public access resulting in disturbance and habitat change by trampling, accidental fire, and so on. It is important to ensure that these factors and the way they influence wildlife are included in our developing research programmes.

The following account does not claim to be a comprehensive assessment of wildlife conservation work throughout Britain today. The variety of subjects is too great for a small book, but we can examine a number of examples which illustrate some of the basic problems of conservation research and the progress which is being made in their study. The views expressed in this book are mainly a personal reflection of my own experience in the management of nature reserves and ecological research, although I owe a great debt to many colleagues for advice and help. In a young, developing subject in which some of the fundamental precepts are scarcely touched by rigorous scientific examination, many different opinions will be found. The subjects discussed in this book should be read in this context; although some order is beginning to emerge and rules and priorities are taking shape, much of the construction work to establish a solid foundation for conservation ecology still lies ahead. Research will provide many of the answers but practical experience, trial and error, and sound common sense also have a vital part to play. Only by advance on all these fronts can we make clear the issues which must form the basis of our policy in the future.

1974   E. D.

Contents

Acknowledgements

I am indebted to my colleagues in the Lowland Grassland Research Section at the Monks Wood Experimental Station, Dr M. G. Morris, T. C. E. Wells, D. A. Wells, Dr L. K. Ward, and Dr J. Sheail, for the privilege of working with them, learning from their research and ideas, and enjoying their stimulating company in the field. All have allowed me to quote their work, but the opinions expressed in this book and any errors it may contain are my responsibility. I am grateful to the following for permission to reproduce photographs and figures: Dr B. Forman, Prof. A. D. Bradshaw, C. S. Elton FRS, Dr F. Perring, Dr N. W. Moore, A. V. Fincham, T. C. E. Wells, Mrs G. Crompton, P. Wakeley, Dr E. van der Maarel, Dr M. Usher, the Nature Conservancy, and the Society for the Promotion of Nature Reserves.

Gordon Mason, M. J. Schofield, and P. C. Tinning have also helped with illustrations and in other ways. In addition I would like to express my thanks to Professor H. M. Thamdrup, University of Aarhus, Denmark, for facilities at the Mols Laboratory, Femmøller.

Lastly I owe a special debt to my wife for helping in many ways with the preparation of the book and for making valuable comments on the text.

1
Wildlife Conservation as an Ecological Problem

The case for state support to conserve wildlife cannot be made entirely on scientific grounds. Legislation to protect our birdlife, byelaws to prohibit the picking of wild flowers, and the establishment of particular areas of country as nature reserves, are motivated as much by a desire to preserve an important part of our natural heritage as for reasons of research and education. The professional biologist and layman alike get the same pleasure from seeing beautiful flowers and insects, rare birds and unusual mammals. The basis, therefore, for a conservation policy is to define what is of value to man in the countryside. Ecologists in the 1940s recognized this when they proposed National Parks for amenity purposes; Educational Nature Reserves; Species Reserves for plants and animals of special interest; and also Habitat Reserves. The last-named included a type of nature reserve which was intended primarily for research purposes.

It was pointed out, however, that *all* reserves were 'habitat' reserves because, whatever their purpose, they had to maintain certain environmental conditions for particular species of plants and animals. It was also clear that many reserves could serve several of these needs, providing that they were big enough and suitably managed, and that access was controlled. Today there are very few reserves which are used solely for research purposes, and in fact certain types of conservation research may best be done on land which has no reserve status. At the other end of the scale a number of reserves have an important amenity and educational function as well as being used for biological study. Examples are certain coastal areas which are a natural focus for the holiday-maker, such as the Oxwich Dunes NNR (National Nature Reserve) in Gower and the Studland Heath NNR in Dorset. Ainsdale Dunes NNR in Lancashire is close to large urban centres and is visited by many thousands of people each year. Blakeney Point, a nature reserve of the National Trust, and Scolt Head NNR, both on the Norfolk coast, are two fine dune systems where research work has been done for over forty years and at the same time large numbers of holiday visitors are able to enjoy seaside amenities. Also in Norfolk are the unique Broads, which form the richest region for fen and water plants and animals in Britain and at the same time attract an increasing number of tourists. The estimated total of 100 000 visitors to this area in 1938 rose to over 270 000 in 1967[2]. In this case the rapid increase is promoted by economic and commercial interests, which bring with them threats to the maintenance of optimum conditions for wildlife on the Broadland National Nature Reserves because of disturbance, pollution, and erosion of banks by the wash from river craft. If we look beyond National Nature Reserves, the Naturalists' Trust reserves and those maintained by the Royal Society for the Protection of Birds, to other types of countryside, there are many areas owned or managed by the National Trust or Local Authorities which were established primarily as Public Open Spaces but which may be valuable conservation areas. Many stretches of coastline, some of the Surrey and Hampshire heaths, Derbyshire dales, woodlands in Wales and the Lake District are good examples.

Modern land use and the survival of wildlife

The rural landscape in a highly developed country such as Britain is the product of a gradual evolution of environmental change in relation to man's cultural and economic activities. As the population multiplies and the standard of living rises, science produces new techniques in agriculture, forestry, land drainage and other forms of land use so that there is a constant flow of new factors which may influence the countryside in ways which are unknown or unpredictable. In the last thirty to forty years these changes have been so rapid (e.g. the disappearance of hedgerows) and sometimes dramatic (widespread use of pesticides) that there is a new public awareness of the deterioration in our environment and the need to study and understand the long-term significance of these events.

Wildlife conservation spans a wide range of scientific and aesthetic needs of man. It promotes scientific research into the problems of understanding the organization of nature which forms the basis of all life and it provides a means of preserving many parts of our countryside heritage which we value. The National Nature Reserve series is an important part of conservation planning but it can never be extensive enough on its own to provide a refuge for the majority of our commoner plants, animals, and birds. The habitats which still survive in the agricultural landscape will therefore be of increasing importance.

No quantitative assessment has been made of the importance of our farmland habitats for conserving wildlife, although some good ecological guesses have been made. The type of countryside which still retains hedge boundaries to most of its fields, with plentiful wayside and field edge trees, numerous ponds, and unmodified streams, is obviously far richer in plants and animals than intensively cultivated land in which hedges and trees have been replaced by wire fences, the ponds filled in, and the field verge reduced to a narrow strip. If, to this, we add the widespread use of pesticides, the opportunity for survival by wildlife is drastically reduced. Between 1933 and 1961 there was a loss of over 2 million acres (833 333 ha) of common land, heath, and moors and an increase from 3.1 to 4.6 million acres (1.3-1.9 million ha) of urban land, and there is evidence too that this trend is accelerating.

It has been calculated that there are about 515 000 acres (214 858 ha) of roads in England and Wales, of which about a third consists of roadside verge. With the building of new roads and widening of existing ones, the acreage of verge is likely to increase and at the present time is equivalent to about three-quarters of that of our statutory nature reserves (National Nature Reserves, Local Nature Reserves, and Forest Nature Reserves). Except for certain rare plants with specialized ecological requirements, most of the common British species can be found on waysides, although the 'quality' of the verge varies very much according to soil type and location. It has been estimated that about fifty species of plants are largely confined to this type of habitat.

Of the different groups of animals, 20 of the 50 species of British mammals, all the 6 species of reptiles, 40 of the 200 breeding birds, 25 of 60 species of butterflies, 8 of 17 species of bumble bees, as well as many other groups, may be regarded as permanent residents of roadsides in different parts of the country. The roadside verge is often much more than a narrow margin of grassland and may include a variety of other habitats which are important refuges for wildlife, such as hedges, ditches, stone walls, woodland strips, earth banks, and extensive steep slopes where the road cuts through railway embankments, several of which have now become Local Nature Reserves following the closure of branch lines.

An estimate by Locke[3] based on sample counts in eight counties gives England, Wales, and Scotland 616 000 miles (985 600 km) of hedgerows, approximately 65 per cent of the total mileage of fields and other types of boundaries. However, measurements from maps and aerial photographs show that hedgerows are disappearing at a rapid rate in several parts of England. This is mainly because mechanized farming finds hedges and trees a hindrance to modern machinery, and pole and wire fences require less maintenance. However, in types of country where pastures still predominate, or where the nature of the country favours small fields, the hedge still survives as the best form of boundary. Good examples can be seen in the West Country. Hedges are also preferred in fox-hunting country because barbed wire can be a dangerous obstacle to horse and rider.

Apart from the changes described, modern agriculture is more efficient when the farming units are large because this permits a greater degree of mechanization and a reduction in the labour force. All this leads to uniformity in the landscape to the detriment of wildlife. In 1953 a survey of birds and animals was made on 70 acres (29 ha) of highly productive farmland in North Norfolk, in which all the fields were cultivated for a cereal crop of sugar beet. The field boundaries were mainly hedgerows but very much reduced in size and height (about 4 ft or 122 cm) and the plough had left only a narrow grass belt two to three feet wide on either side. Very few trees survived in the hedges, whose main function was to provide cover for partridges. The survey showed that the bird life consisted of only three common breeding species: the partridge, the skylark and the lapwing, and the only common mammal was the hare. A few wood pigeons and yellow buntings were recorded but the thin, low hedges would be a poor environment for the familiar breeding birds of better hedgerows elsewhere[4].

In contrast to this, an eight-year study of the breeding birds on a mixed farm of 220 acres (91.6 ha) in Suffolk showed a remarkably rich fauna[5]. The farm included deciduous and coniferous woodland and scrub, 4½ miles (7.2 km) of hedgerow with trees, small ponds, and a shelterbelt, and about a third was under a grass ley, the remainder with cereal and root crops. Modern fertilizer and spraying practices were used but with regard to wildlife. During the eight years, 42 species of birds bred or held territory every year and a further 24 bred on one occasion or more. The mean population density was estimated at 280 pairs per 100 acres (41.6 ha), a total which can only be attained where there is a good deal of habitat variety.

The ecological problem of conserving Britain's wildlife is therefore much greater than establishing a series of nature reserves. Wildlife does not recognize the boundaries of protected areas, and even with the support of legislation such as the Bird Protection Acts, without suitable nesting sites, food uncontaminated with pesticides, and freedom from disturbance, many birds would decline in numbers. Much wildlife is still unprotected by state laws, particularly non-game mammals, reptiles and amphibia, and wild plants which do not grow on reserves or where there are no local byelaws which make it an offence to collect them. The same applies to Britain's wealth of invertebrate life. The contribution which different types of land can make to wildlife conservation will be discussed in Chapter 2.

2
Land Use History and Wildlife

Many of the classical studies on British vegetation during the last fifty years have been made on areas where disturbance and modification have been generally less than elsewhere, for example Wicken Fen, near Cambridge, the Breckland heaths, salt marshes, mountains, raised bogs, and some forests. The ecological principles which developed during this period, particularly on succession, community structure, phytosociology and the influence of soils, aspect, water regime, and climate on plants, were all important factors used to define the scientific status of sites and the selection of nature reserves. Although this was the wisest approach to take because the range of ecological variation could be defined within each major formation, great importance was initially placed on 'naturalness'. The influence of man was regarded as an intrusion which had no place in scientific conservation, and areas which had been greatly modified by him were considered to be of lower status. Few conservationists still hold this view today and it is accepted that man is, and has been for many centuries, part of the rural environment, however unspoilt it may appear, and that he will continue to modify, in some way, each place to which he has access. Rather than assessing sites according to supposed naturalness, it is now believed that we should study in greater detail the changes in the fauna and flora brought about by human activities so that we can reconstruct past events and predict changes in the future.

The discovery of the artificial origin of the Norfolk Broads[6] was probably the first well-documented example of a study in ecological history, and since then detailed work has been done on Lakenheath Warren in Breckland, on certain ancient woodlands, and on that very important common animal, the rabbit. So far this new subject has been mainly concerned with documentary records, but field evidence is now being studied much more closely, aided by archaeology and aerial photography.

Of particular importance to the ecologist is the nature of disturbance and modification to the natural environment during the last 200 years or so. This is a short space of time to the historian but it covers the period of the Industrial Revolution, a rapid increase in population, and wars which depleted our timber resources and stimulated the drainage of marshes and reclamation of old pasture. Studies of this period tend to show that changes due to exploitation and disturbance were greater than previously suspected. For example, Lakenheath Warren in the Suffolk Breckland was a sheep walk from at least Roman times and this was combined with rabbit warrening from the second half of the thirteenth century to the early twentieth century, when sheep rearing began to decline[7]. Until 1942, when the western half was incorporated in an airfield, the Warren had retained its shape and size—about 2300 acres (958.3 ha)—for centuries, partly because it was in church ownership for over 600 years (to 1870) and partly because common rights held by local villagers were strongly defended. All these factors helped to prevent major changes in land use, but careful study has shown that the recent history of the Warren includes local ploughing, extensive gravel and sand extraction, use by the army for training and artillary practice, disturbance and dumping of soil for the creation of target areas, and damage to vegetation by the use of heavy vehicles such as tanks. On one extensive area, for instance, a vegetation cover of lichens was destroyed by tank training exercises and the site was subsequently colonized by heather.

Woodland history

Until recently woodlands have been much neglected by historians, particularly detailed studies of individual forest areas. It has often been assumed by forest botanists that many surviving British woodlands are related to floristically comparable forests of the later post-glacial period, but definite evidence has been lacking. This point is of considerable importance for conservation because secondary woodlands, planted by man, may remain poor floristically—and presumably faunistically—for centuries. However, where it can be shown that woodland cover has remained unbroken for a very long period, archaeological and biological evidence of past management may also have been preserved. For example, ditches and other surface features such as boundary banks, particularly on heavy land, are easily traced, as are foundations of old buildings or the ridge-and-furrow of old arable land. Other important historical clues are found in the spacing and species of trees present, counts of growth rings, pollarding, and the woodland structure of canopy, large and small coppice[8]. Further evidence can be obtained from the presence of assemblages of plants which appear to be characteristic of ancient woodlands, for example, the oxlip (*Primula elatior*), wild service tree (*Sorbus torminalis*), small-leaved lime (*Tilia cordata*), bats-in-the-belfry (*Campanula trachelium*), dog's mercury (*Mercurialis perennis*) and greater butterfly orchid (*Platanthera chlorantha*). Secondary woodland can sometimes be recognized by the presence of such species as spurge laurel (*Daphne laureola*), cowslip (*Primula veris*) and cow parsley (*Anthriscus sylvestris*). Some species of lichens have also been shown to be largely confined to ancient woodland, growing on large old trees, particularly oaks. Pollen analysis has been used in Denmark to trace the history of the Draved forest in Jutland, but in Britain suitable deposits in woodlands seem to be rare.

There are many documentary sources available to the historical ecologist. The first Ordnance Survey maps for the first half of the nineteenth century may be of special value in tracing woodland boundaries but land use information is very generalized. Large-scale enclosure, tithe and estate maps are usually better sources of information. They were used in the example of the Woodbastwick Marshes (page 32) and for the study of Lakenheath Warren. National land surveys, the most famous being the Doomsday Book of 1086, are also consulted. Other sources are estate surveys concerned with wills, leases, conveyances, annual accounts of estates which contained particulars of timber and coppice sold, and law suits about woodlands which required a detailed survey of the timber and forest management. A document of special value is the Hundred Rolls, a detailed though imperfectly preserved national survey of 1279. This recorded the extent of woodland in each parish but not the location. In Cambridgeshire, for example, it has been shown that the eleven parishes on boulder clay which contained woodland in 1279 are, with one exception, the same parishes which contain ancient woodland today[8].

A similar history can be traced for a number of well-known forest areas, although detailed studies of land use are few. The New Forest and Windsor Forest are examples, but one of the most interesting is Wytham Wood in Berkshire, a few miles north of Oxford[9]. Here the University owns an estate of 3400 acres (1416.5 ha), of which about a third consists of woodland and scrub situated on twin limestone hills in a loop of the river Thames. For twenty-five years the woodland fauna and flora has been studied by a succession of post-graduate ecologists from Oxford, encouraged, guided, and supervised by Charles Elton, the distinguished animal ecologist. In 1966 Elton brought together the accumulated data of this work in his book *The Pattern of Animal Communities,* making Wytham Wood the best documented forest area for animal life in the country, and establishing a base-line against which other faunal surveys can be assessed[10]. Forest land has survived on the Wytham Hills since pre-Conquest times, although like other woodland areas it has been greatly modified by a succession of different ownerships and by common rights of grazing before enclosure. Elton sums this up by saying: 'By no stretch of the imagination can Wytham Hill be called an entirely natural ecosystem; its rocks quarried for road metal, its timber selectively cut down or pollarded, its oak bark taken for tanning, its dead wood gathered for fuel, its glades cattle-grazed, its predatory animals and birds shot to protect game, some parts deforested for croplands, or heavily scarred by recent forestry fellings and plantings, some fields allowed to grow back into woodland . . .'.

It has been shown in a number of instances that very old woodlands often have a distinctive flora and fauna, including rare species with specialized requirements which may be easily eliminated by habitat disturbance or modification. For example, the ancient woodland of Staverton Park and The Thicks in East Suffolk has probably maintained a tree cover since before the Doomsday survey[11]. Only native species of trees occur in the wood (notably oak, holly, birch, rowan and elm), the oldest living trees (oaks) being well over 400 years old. Except for the birds, the fauna has not been well studied, but the lichen flora is particularly rich for an East Anglian woodland of this size, sixty-four species having been recorded. Dr Francis Rose, who did most of the field work on these plants, comments (*loc. cit.*): 'This assemblage of species suggests very clearly to me that Staverton Park and The Thicks is almost certainly a relict of ancient forest cover in this part of England and that there has been here a fair degree of permanence of forest conditions and tree cover and lack of any major clear felling and replanting. Many of these species, to judge from their present known distributions, and what is known from historical records, are ill-adapted to change and today are normally unable to colonize new and isolated habitats in Britain, even in areas of low air pollution. They are largely confined to old trees and appear to be relict in nature, though where larger areas of old forest still exist, e.g. the New Forest, they seem able still to colonize younger but mature trees and so to maintain themselves. Their ultimate fate at

Staverton may depend therefore on encouragement of regeneration or on planting of younger oaks to 'take over' in due course.'

Three years earlier Elton had considered the same points in relation to animals in Wytham but suggested that if the wood was in a region where other forest land was common, such a situation might be as important a factor as a long history without major disturbance. As an example he refers to three locally rare species: the ant *Lasius brunneus,* the beetle *Prionychus ater,* and the centipede *Crytops hortensis.* All three were recorded in rotting beech trees originally planted about 150 years ago on land which was formerly farm fields. Adjacent to the beech is a woodland with a much longer history dating back to the Middle Ages. These three species have not yet been recorded for the latter area, probably because most of the large old trees were cut out some years ago. In fact nearly all so-called relict ancient forest animal species are associated with large old trees which include a good deal of dead wood. This particular microhabitat may well be a more important factor for the survival of such species than continuity of forest conditions for many centuries.

The spiders *Lepthyphantes carri* (Linyphiidae) and *Tetrilus macrophthalmus* (Agelenidae) are interesting examples of ancient forest species because, unlike most rare beetles associated with old timber, they are not dependent on rotten wood for food material. *L. carri,* which is not known outside Britain, has been recorded only in the ancient woodlands of Windsor Forest, Epping Forest, Sherwood Forest, and Donnington Park (on the north side of Charnwood Forest in Leicester-shire). Although several specimens have been taken in rotten wood and accumulated leaf litter inside large hollow trees, it has also occurred in woodpigeon and jackdaw nests, on the bark of a tree and even under a piece of bark on the ground. *T. macrophthalmus* is more widespread but is typically found in cracks and galleries in soft rotten wood in large old trees. Nevertheless in Charnwood Forest it has an alternative habitat under large heavy stones embedded in ground vegetation and frequently in association with ants. Mr John Crocker has discovered it in these situations at several sites where it seems to survive after the ancient woodland has almost entirely been cut down. *Pelecopsis bicapitata,* a rare spider described from Poland and Czechoslovakia, seems to be a similar example[73]. This species occurs in relict deciduous mountain forests and occupies a very restricted habitat among the crevices in the bark and between superficial roots around the base, and lower part of the trunk, of old oak trees. The species avoids the leaf litter on the ground between the trees and seems to be very localized even in favourable woodland habitats.

The scarcity of these species and of many insects of dead wood today is because very few present-day woodlands, whatever their history, have large old trees in a state of decay; it is a habitat which requires two centuries or more to develop. Ancient woodland is usually more diverse, structurally, than young woodland and this may be reflected in a larger number of species in some groups of insects. Windsor Great Forest has a list of beetles which reaches almost 2000 species (over half the known British fauna); the New Forest scores about 1200, Epping Forest 1114, Wytham Wood 1078, while the Monks Wood NNR, where it is likely that forest cover has been maintained since at least the early Middle Ages, has 944 species recorded. However, comparisons of this sort are of very limited value because we do not know how large an area was worked by the early collectors. For example, today Windsor Forest and Park extends over 7800 acres (3250 ha), which includes 3000 acres (1250 ha) of oak woodland and many other habitats as well. Nevertheless, in the last century collectors seem to have roamed over a much larger area, probably nearer 28 000 acres (11 666 ha). On the other hand Monks Wood is now reduced to only 387 acres (161.2 ha), although forty years ago much rough pasture and scrub (now ploughed) surrounded the wood and was visited by collectors.

Hedgerow history

Species richness is of course often achieved by the passage of time. A newly planted woodland of only two to three species will be colonized by other trees and shrubs, while a new grass ley, even though grazed or mown, provides a habitat for other herbs and grasses if left long enough without ploughing. A particularly interesting example is the history of hedgerows. The disappearance of hedges in many parts of the country has attracted a good deal of research on their origin and on the plants and animals which live in them. Although many hedges were planted during the extensive enclosures of the eighteenth and nineteenth centuries, others are known to follow very ancient boundaries. By combining field studies with an examination of old documents and maps for 227 different hedges, work at Monks Wood Experimental Station[12] showed that, in general, the older the hedge the greater were the number of species of woody plants. The average rate of recruitment was worked out at one species every hundred years, so that a hedge with ten species (based on sample lengths of 30 yards:27.6 m) would be about a thousand years old. The actual figure is in fact somewhere between 900 and 1130 years, because there is a fairly wide range of variation due to different soils, climatic conditions, local traditions, and hedge management. Interesting regional differences also occur. For instance, in Kent hedges with only one species are rare, but hedges with 3, 4 or 5 species are relatively common. In the counties of Huntingdon and Lincoln most hedges have 1, 2 or 3 species, but in Devon over a quarter of the hedges seem to be over 800 years old and the data suggest that there was a good deal of enclosure 700 years ago, coinciding, perhaps, with the agricultural expansion of the thirteenth century.

Further evidence on the age of hedgerows has been obtained by a study of the commonest hedgerow plants, the hawthorns[13]. There are two species in Britain, the common hawthorn (*Crataegus monogyna*) and the midland hawthorn (*C. laevigata*), the former being more widespread and having divided leaves, one style, and one stone in the fruit, while the latter has almost entire leaves, two or more styles, and two stones in the fruit. *C. monogyna* is the characteristic hawthorn of open situations occurring outside woodland and having the growth form of a typical scrub plant. It is, for instance, commonly found as an invader of neglected grassland. By contrast, *C. laevigata* is found mostly in woodlands on heavy clays, where it grows well under the canopy of trees. Although obviously good species, they hybridize freely and many populations can be found which combine the characters of both and are also perfectly fertile. Presumably under natural conditions their different ecological preferences kept them apart, but under the disturbed conditions of a man-made landscape this type of isolation is broken down.

Some evidence of this process can be seen by comparing some of our ancient hedgerows with more recent ones. Today quickset hedges are planted almost entirely with *C. monogyna* and the same species seems to have been propagated for the numerous new hedges created during the time of the Enclosure Acts. Much earlier, however, it seems likely that hedges were planted with cuttings from the nearest available source of hawthorn, and these would often have been *C. laevigata*. In other cases, hedgerows on new boundaries may have been formed by leaving bushes and trees along a woodland edge, the remainder of the forest being cleared. Such a hedge would also tend to have more *C. laevigata*. In Figure 2 the two species, distinguished by measuring leaf indentation, were sampled in hedges of different ages near the Monks Wood NNR.

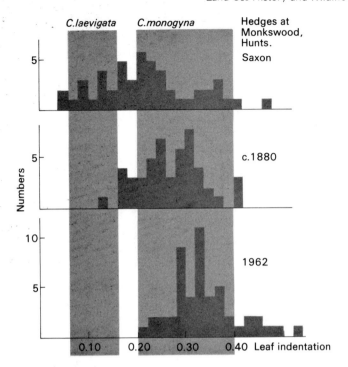

Figure 2. Histogram of leaf indentation of populations of *Crataegus* in hedgerows of different ages. Beside Saxon Road, Monks Wood, Huntingdon. [Bradshaw[13]]

The Saxon hedge shows that the process of hybridization has progressed to an advanced stage because most of the plants show characteristics intermediate between the two species. The nineteenth century hedge is mainly *C. monogyna* but also with intermediate forms, while the modern hedge is entirely of this species. There is also an interesting distribution of both species in Monks Wood itself. The commonest species, as would be expected, is *C. laevigata,* but in the south-east corner of this ancient woodland *C. monogyna* and intermediate forms prevail. In the same areas there is clear evidence of ridge and furrow of past cultivation. When the land was abandoned and allowed to revert to woodland again the open conditions favoured *C. monogyna,* which has survived to the present day, although it is likely to give way to *C. laevigata* in the course of time.

Grassland history

Ever since neolithic man began to clear the forests which covered virtually the whole of lowland Britain at that time, there has been a gradual expansion of grassland as more land was cleared for cultivation and grazing. Today over 62 per cent of the land surface consists of grassland, the larger proportion being rough grazings and permanent pastures on the hills and moors of northern and south-west England, Wales, and Scotland. The long history of use of grasslands by man is demonstrated by archaeological evidence, such as camp sites, burial mounds, trackways, and settlements[14]. Many of these surface features have probably never been ploughed and the turf is consequently of considerable scientific interest. However, in most cases subsequent management such as intensive grazing has greatly modified the plant community and, although recent studies have been made, we do not yet understand the relationship between floristic composition and age of grassland. Some plants with exacting ecological requirements, for example the scarce pasque flower *Pulsatilla vulgaris,* which occurs on calcareous soils, has been shown to survive heavy grazing, annual burning, trampling, and competition from the vigorous growth of coarse grasses[15]. Its marked decline during the last 200 years has been largely due to the ploughing of old grassland where it occurs rather than to type of management. It appears to be a species which is very slow to re-establish on soils which have been allowed to revert to grassland following cultivation. One exception is a well-known colony of the pasque flower at Barnack Hills and Holes in Northamptonshire. This site is known to have been a limestone quarry in Roman times and continued to be worked until at least the Middle Ages and from time to time afterwards. The plant now grows in grassland which has developed on the old spoil heaps of quarry waste.

Evidence of ploughing at some time in the past is therefore of considerable importance to the grassland conservation ecologist. The familiar ridge and furrow, or 'hills and hollocks', as it is sometimes called, is the best known feature and commonly seen in meadows of lowland England, particularly on heavy land. Unfortunately the dating of this relict of ploughing is difficult, although the greater distance between adjacent ridges is thought by some historians to indicate greater age. In some meadows, for example those at Upwood in Huntingdonshire (Figure 3), which have a spendidly rich flora, the ridges and furrows have a reversed S-shape and it has been suggested that this came about at a

Figure 3. Upwood Meadows, Huntingdonshire. Snow lying in the furrows clearly shows the reversed S-shape on the 'ridge and furrow' denoting ancient ploughing. [*Photo T. C. E. Wells*]

time when ploughing was done with ox-teams. As the team approached the edge of the field it began to turn rather early and always to the left, because of ease of manoeuvring, and this produced curved ends to the ridges and furrows which are visible today. Another well-known feature of ancient ploughing is the so-called Celtic fields of Saxon origin, widespread on the chalklands of southern England (Figure 4). The excellent state of preservation of many Celtic fields suggests that they may not have been ploughed subsequently. Parsonage Down on the Wiltshire chalk is a good example and of special interest because it has a very rich flora.

It is clear that there are many unanswered questions in the ecological history of grassland. Documentary evidence can be of great value, particularly the use of maps and papers referring to an individual estate. But unlike woodlands, whose tree species are often described in old documents because of their economic value, the botanical composition of grassland is seldom mentioned. The contrast is greater in the case of

Figure 4. Celtic fields, Shillingstone Hill, Dorset, 1949—now all destroyed by ploughing. [*Photo J. K. St. Joseph, Cambridge University Collection: Copyright reserved*]

field evidence. Woodlands preserve the history of their association with man in the forest structure and growth form of the trees as well as in disturbance to the forest floor. On the other hand, grasslands may go through many different forms of land use without much evidence surviving on the ground surface. Perhaps, however, much information is still present in the soil structure and soil chemistry and in the plant life, but we have not yet learned what we must look for in the way of historical clues. This is still a very new subject and significant advances can be expected in the future which will be of great benefit to conservation studies.

3
The Nature Reserve and its Landscape Environment

In the last chapter we followed the evolution of the nature reserve through the course of history and tried to understand how the fauna and flora had been influenced by events of the past. In the more remote areas of the country where traditional ways of rural life have persisted, the rate of change has been slower and differences between the nature reserve and the agricultural landscape in which it is set are reduced or even scarcely noticeable. But in some lowland regions, on richer land, where mechanization is fully developed and high economic returns are demanded, the nature reserve is a conspicuous and isolated piece of land often in a potentially hostile environment. The purpose of this chapter is to examine a few examples of reserves, singly and in groups, which illustrate some of the problems of survival in a modern landscape moulded by the demands of technology, tourism, agriculture, and increasing numbers of people.

The East Anglian Breckland

Sandy heathland areas are well known in lowland England but perhaps the most distinctive and best studied is the Breckland region of south-west Norfolk and north-west Suffolk. The term 'Breck' referred to the 'breaking' of land for periodic cultivation which ceased when the light soils were exhausted of nutrients and the land was allowed to revert to heath again. The sandy soils, which are of glacial and interglacial origin, extend over nearly 250 000 acres (104 166 ha), although most are now cultivated or forest-covered. After the sands had been deposited following the retreat of the glaciers, it seems likely that a forest— probably mainly of oak—eventually developed over the area. When neolithic man arrived, he found that the soils were easy to cultivate and the tree cover was gradually destroyed. Since that time the open heaths have been virtually treeless until the planting of windbreaks began in the early nineteenth century and the extensive afforestation in the twentieth century. In the centuries between, sheep-grazing was the traditional land use of the dry grassland and heath, and the familiar rabbit—not known in Britain before the Norman conquest—was scarce outside the warrens until the seventeenth and eighteenth centuries. With the breaking up of the warrens at this time, the rabbit rapidly became a serious agricultural pest and remained so until 1954, when the myxoma virus destroyed almost the whole population in two to three years.

In many places, particularly where there is only a thin layer over the underlying chalk, the soils may be very calcareous with pH values of about 8.0. Where the sand is much deeper, the chalk fragments have been leached out, leaving an acid sand which is often dominated by heather instead of grass. The Breckland plateau is dissected by four river valleys, the Lark, Wissey, Thet, and Little Ouse, and scattered throughout the northern part of the region are several small land-locked lakes, the famous Breckland meres. The meres and the valley fens have their own distinctive flora and fauna and, although only fragments survive today, they are of special biogeographical importance because of their situation on the edge of the Fenland Basin, with Reserves such as Woodwalton Fen, Holme Fen, and Wicken Fen to the west, and the Norfolk Broads to the north-east, both outstanding areas with important differences in vegetation and animal life.

The climatic characteristics of Breckland are nearer to semi-continental conditions than elsewhere in Europe, and this, combined with the light porous soils, is responsible for its outstanding wildlife interest. The meteorological data from Cambridge—situated to the south-west of Breckland, but in the same climatic region—from Santon Downham in the heart of Breckland, and from the coastal town of Gorleston, 42 miles (67.2 km) to the east, help to illustrate the Breck's distinctive climate. Average annual rainfall over much of the area is about 610 mm, ranging from 559 in the west to between 610 and 635 in the east and south, and 635 and 686 in the north. In addition to this modest rainfall, Breckland has a high potential soil moisture deficit during the summer months, averaging 152 mm from April to September. Table 1 shows that average monthly temperatures are higher in the summer than on the coast and lower in the winter, while the annual maxima and minima are more extreme. There is also a much greater frequency of ground frosts than in other parts of the country—Santon Downham, for instance, recording frosts in each month of the year during the period 1960-1964.

The types of grassland and heaths in Breckland have been intensively studied for many years, particularly the relationship between the plant

Table 1. Meteorological records for Breckland and the East Coast.

(a) Mean number of days when summer temperature exceeded 20.1°C (68.0°F) for period 1956-65.

	Gorleston	Cambridge
May	0.6	6.0
June	4.5	15.0
July	7.5	18.0
August	7.6	16.8

(b) Annual total of days with ground frost.

	Gorleston	Cambridge	Breckland
1955	68	109	130 (Thetford)
1956	68	102	143 (Thetford)
1957	33	90	
1958	51	100	
1959	39	102	
1960	29	91	128 (Santon Downham)
1961	44	95	184 (Santon Downham)
1962	83	158	185 (Santon Downham)
1963	88	140	166 (Santon Downham)
1964	52	131	166 (Santon Downham)
Mean	55	112	157

communities and the soils, which range from highly calcareous to deeper leached sands. The distinctive flora includes many species associated with continental steppe conditions and there is a high proportion of annuals which need open, disturbed ground to survive. The richest flora and the best known rarities are found on the more base-rich soils: field southernwood (*Artemisia campestris*), spiked speedwell (*Veronica spicata*), spring speedwell (*V. verna*), *V. praecox*, fingered speedwell (*V. triphyllos*), Spanish catchfly (*Silene otites*), striated catchfly (*S. conica*), glabrous rupture-wort (*Herniaria glabra*), Böhmer's cat's tail (*Phleum phleioides*), sickle medick (*Medicago falcata*), small medick (*M. minima*), wall bedstraw (*Galium parisiense*), wild thyme (*Thymus serpyllum* ssp. *serpyllum*), perennial knawel (*Scleranthus perennis* ssp. *prostratus*), *Crassula tillaea*, *Carex ericetorum* and grape hyacinth (*Muscari atlanticum*). Several northern plants also find their most southerly station in Breckland: the moss *Rhytidium rugosum* grows on the open Brecks, while the orchid, creeping lady's tresses (*Goodyera repens*), and the mosses *Dicranum rugosum* and *Ptilium crista-castrensis* occur in the conifer plantations, of which over 46 000 acres (19 166 ha) have been planted since 1920.

The vertebrate fauna of Breckland, particularly the birds and mammals, has been well documented in the annual reports of the Norfolk and Norwich Natural History Society, the Suffolk Naturalists' Society and the Cambridge Natural History Society. The extensive conifer plantations have provided a new habitat for the red and roe deer, which are now comparatively numerous and are tolerated by the Forestry Commission providing damage to young trees can be prevented. These forests also form a stronghold for the native red squirrel, which is more widespread here than anywhere else in East Anglia. On the meres and fens the wild duck population includes the scarce gadwall and garganey among the regular breeding species, and from time to time the Montague's harrier has bred. In the years prior to 1962 the introduced coypu spread from the Norfolk Broads into the wetlands of the Breck, but the severe winter of that year destroyed the population and, fortunately, no reinvasion has yet taken place.

Prior to 1954 the enormous rabbit population on the heaths was the most important single factor maintaining the characteristic disturbed ground and short vegetation. This animal was also an important crop for meat and fur (felt-making for hats); see Figure 5. After the virtual destruction of the population by myxomatosis, the surge of vegetation growth greatly altered the appearance and character of the heaths. The bare sandy areas became vegetated, the rabbit holes filled in and gorse and young conifers began to spread over the open land. The habitat of the rare annual plants became very scarce and most of the typical heathland birds, particularly the stone curlew, woodlark, wheatear, and ringed plover, declined in numbers. The red-backed shrike, stonechat, and nightjar also became much scarcer but in these cases the decline appears to be part of a general recession over most of the country. On the credit side was an increase in the numbers of the common curlew, which colonized the heathlands as the heather and grass grew up to provide sheltered nest-sites.

The comparative ease with which this trend can be reversed can be seen on the Weeting Heath NNR in Norfolk. Vegetation change on this calcareous heath after 1954 almost eliminated the stone curlew and wheatear as breeding species. Small areas of heathland were mown and others rotavated in an attempt to provide nest-sites for the former, and drain-pipes were sunk into the ground to simulate rabbit burrows

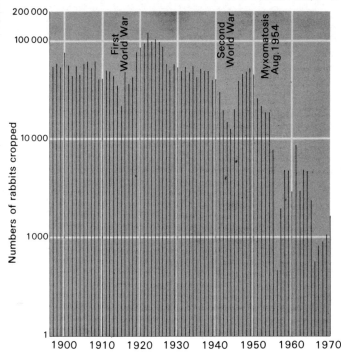

Figure 5. The rabbit crop taken on the Elveden Estate, Breckland, from 1896 to 1970. [*After Crompton*[7]]

required by the latter. Neither was successful. Then in 1959 a 40-acre (16.6 ha) area was fenced to enclose a remnant of the rabbit population, preventing contact with diseased animals outside. The population increased rapidly, cropped down the vegetation and, by scratching and burrowing, restored pre-myxomatosis Breckland conditions (see Figure 6). Both stone curlew and wheatear returned as regular breeding species, and invertebrate species of open-ground habitats also increased in numbers. Myxomatosis was not completely excluded from the enclosed population but outbreaks were less frequent than on outside areas and recovery was usually rapid.

The invertebrate fauna of Breckland is not as well known as the plant and vertebrate life, but nevertheless has been fairly well worked in recent

Figure 6. Weeting Heath NNR, Norfolk. Pine regeneration is prevented in the rabbit enclosure (on right) but is widespread outside where rabbits are scarce. [*Photo B. Forman*]

years, particularly on the heaths and in the fens. The mobile inland dunes provide conditions for the so-called maritime elements in the fauna, arenaceous species which are typically associated with coastal dunes. The beetle *Broscus cephalotes,* a species characteristic of the driftline on sandy beaches, has not been seen in recent years, but the dune wolf-spider *Arctosa perita* and the jumping spider *Attulus saltator* are still present, although local. A number of other invertebrates are rare heathland species which, although occurring in other parts of the country, are particularly well-established in Breckland. Another feature of interest is the association of rare insects with common plants, so that the weeds of abandoned fields, wasteland, and roadside in Breckland are of special conservation importance. The bug *Arenocoris waltlii* and the beetle *Phytonomus dauci* both feed on the common storksbill (*Erodium cicutarium*) (common on coastal dunes), but neither insect has been taken outside Breckland. The moth *Lithostege griseata* and the weevil *Ceuthorhynchus pulvinatus* feed on flixweed (*Descurainia sophia*) but are not known outside Breckland. The moth *Emmelia trabealis* feeds on the common bindweed (*Convulvulus arvensis*) but has seldom been taken elsewhere in Britain. On the Breckland poplars there occur the very local moth *Cirrhia ocellaris*, and the rare weevils *Dorytomus tremulae* and *D. filirostris;* broom and Scots pine also have rare species associated with them.

On the roadside verges the weevil *Ceuthorhynchus unguicularis* is found on the hairy rock-cress (*Arabis hirsuta*) and occurs in only one other locality in England. Some of the rare plants also have interesting and very local species feeding on them as, for example, the moth *Anepia irregularis*, whose larvae feed on the seed heads of the Spanish catchfly (*Silene otites*), both insect and plant occurring only in Breckland.

The fens and open waters which provide habitats for some very distinctive invertebrate species are of four types: eutrophic valley mires; land-locked meres, some with markedly fluctuating water tables; mesotrophic basin mires, developed on extinct mires; and numerous small meres and mires which may have formed in pits and hollows now thought to be late glacial ground-ice depressions. The spider fauna of this fragmentary but important complex has affinities with the Fen Basin sites, particularly Wicken Fen, and with the much more extensive wetlands of the Norfolk Broads. It has in fact more rarities than either, although the status of several is becoming precarious.

Most of the Breck fens are small areas and many attempts have been made in the past to reclaim them for agricultural use. A few have survived major change, either because they had common land status or else because the terrain, such as the many water-filled depressions on Foulden Common, made a change of use very difficult. Others have been severely affected by modern technology, particularly those situated within the influence of the new flood relief cut-off channel which extends for 27 miles (45 km) from the River Lark near Mildenhall to Denver Sluice south of Kings Lynn. This channel has lowered the ground water-table two to three feet (60-90 cm) on nearby land so that some fenlands and previously wet meadows could be ploughed for the first time in the early 1960s.

The impact of these changes on the fauna is normally difficult to assess, except perhaps in terms of notable rarities which may disappear. In 1969 and 1970 an extensive survey of the spider fauna of eleven Breckland fen sites was made and the results analysed statistically[16]. The dendogram produced (Figure 7) shows that the eleven sites fall into three groups, groups A and B being more similar to each other than either is to group C. Examination of the location of the areas studied shows that groups A and B are both valley fens situated by the Breck rivers while

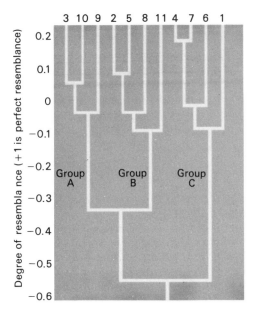

Figure 7. Dendogram showing relationships between the spider fauna of eleven East Anglian fens, based on species and numbers taken in 88 one-hour recording periods (8 hours per site). Group A species-poor valley fens; much disturbed. Group B species-rich valley fens; little disturbed. Group C moderately species-rich isolated fens.

group C sites are scattered, isolated fens away from the river valleys. Of particular interest, however, is the separation of the valley fens into a species-poor group (A) where considerable disturbance to vegetation or water table had taken place, and a species-rich group (B), where interference by man appeared to have been much less. Foulden Common, Norfolk, one of the richest sites studied, at first appeared to be an exception to this general conclusion. The fen areas at Foulden are confined to a series of relatively small depressions which could easily be regarded as human artefacts created by excavation for marl or other mineral resource. However, recent research has shown that these water-filled pits are probably natural phenomena attributable to the formation of ground ice during the Late-glacial (Weichselian) and its subsequent thawing[74].

The creation of a large man-made forest in Breckland, after 1920, destroyed many of the extensive heathlands, and at the same time

Figure 8. East Wretham Heath, Breckland.

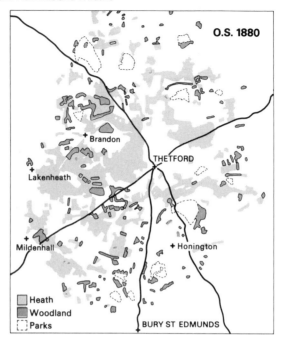

Figure 9(a). Land use in Breckland in 1880.

progress in agricultural science made it possible to cultivate land which
was previously regarded as too poor. Much of the open heathland was
ploughed up, particularly during the 1930s and 1940s, only fragments
surviving to the post-war years. Some measure of the decline in
heathland during the last ninety or so years can be obtained from a
comparison of Breckland maps for 1880 and 1968 (Figure 9). The
estimate of 54 000 acres (22 500 ha) of Breck heaths in 1880 must be
regarded as very approximate because contemporary maps had
insufficient data to reconstruct land use in detail. Today about 1600
acres (666 ha) of heath survive on nature reserves and 5000 acres
(2083 ha) on private properties and commons, together with 12 500
acres (5208 ha) on Ministry of Defence land. In 1880 it is estimated that
there were about 59 separate areas averaging 916 acres (381 ha) each,
while in 1968 the number has been reduced to 37 sites with an average
size of 86 acres (35.8 ha). The latter figure excludes the large area of
farmland now used for training purposes. The loss of heathland during

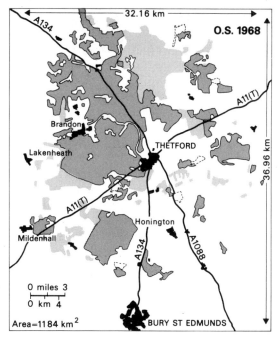

Figure 9(b). Land use in Breckland in 1968.

this period is therefore about 70 per cent, roughly the same as that for the Dorset heaths between 1811 and 1960 (page 50)[17].

In summary we can say that the main environmental factors influencing wildlife on Breckland reserves are reduction in size, fragmentation and isolation brought about by extensive afforestation and agricultural reclamation, drainage of wetlands, vegetation change and spread of scrub following elimination of the rabbit as a major biotic influence, new habitats (man-made forests) bringing in a new fauna and flora, and the destruction of the important weed flora and fauna by efficient farming techniques. A factor which has not been mentioned is the effect of man as a visitor. Although tourists visit the Breck reserves, particularly at weekends, they are mostly local people, and disturbance, if it is important, is probably caused as much by the numerous bird-watchers as by the general public. Tourism, as an industry, has not yet developed, but in our next case study, the Norfolk Broads, it has become one of the most significant of man's activities affecting wildlife.

The Norfolk Broads

In the flat land of eastern Norfolk and adjacent parts of Suffolk between
Norwich and the coast are the valleys of the Thurne, Ant, Bure, Wensum,
and Waveney, all draining into the sea at Great Yarmouth. In the upper
and middle reaches of these valleys, particularly the first three, forty-six
lakes, or Broads, occur, varying in size from small and shallow to
impressive expanses of open water covering more than 300 acres
(125 ha). The total surface area of water is nearly 2000 acres (833 ha),
well over half of which is open to public navigation, the remainder being
either too shallow for boats, private, or inaccessible from the rivers[2].

The landscape of the Broads, with fringing reedswamp and fen
scrublands of alder carr, looks as near natural as one could find in
lowland England, and, indeed, until 1952 these lakes were thought to
have developed naturally in the upper parts of the river valleys just
beyond a thick wedge of estuarine clay deposited by a marine incursion
in Romano-British times. Then in the early 1950s the Norfolk botanist,
Dr J. M. Lambert, discovered that the Broads had steep sides of solid
peat, unlike the shore lines of natural lakes, and that the flat bottoms
were covered with a loose, soft mud, quite different from the material of
the 'ronds' (the solid peatland separating the Broads from the rivers[6]).
No known natural agency could have produced the lake bottom profiles
characteristic of the Broads, and Dr Lambert concluded that they were
in fact artificial lakes originating from enormous man-made peat cuttings
excavated for fuel.

The theory raised many difficult historical and archaeological
questions, but after several years of patient investigation historians were
able to show that for a period of about 350 years, from approximately
the tenth to fourteenth centuries, vast quantities of peat were dug from
these valleys. In fact with an original area of 3000 acres (1250 ha), and
an average depth of 8 ft (2.5 m), although many are deeper, well over 9
hundred million cubic feet of peat (25.2 million m^3) must have been
removed. The final problem in this remarkable story was to explain how
it was possible to excavate such large pits to a depth of 10 ft (3 m) or
more without them becoming flooded. An archaeologist and a civil
engineer who were working on deposits in the Great Yarmouth area (the
outfall of the Broadland rivers) discovered pottery and other materials
which showed that in the thirteenth century the Yarmouth spit stood
about 13 ft (4 m) higher above the sea than it does now. By the close of
the thirteenth century submergence had begun, and progressive lowering

Figure 10. Aerial photograph of Sutton Broad showing old shoreline and encroachment of primary fen. [*Photo J. K. St. Joseph, Cambridge University Collection: Copyright reserved*]

of the land surface in relation to sea level caused the pits to become flooded, creating what we now call the Norfolk Broads.

In the course of time silt accumulated in the Broads, so that in the shallower ones marsh vegetation was able to grow out from the margins and open water disappeared. The aerial photograph of Sutton Broad in Figure 10 clearly shows the contrast between the marsh vegetation covering the former water surface and the alder/sallow carr growing on the firm uncut peat of the margins. Successional changes of this type, varying according to size and depth of the original peat cutting, influenced by the nature of the adjacent vegetation and the use made of the marshland, created a very diverse range of habitats (Figure 11).

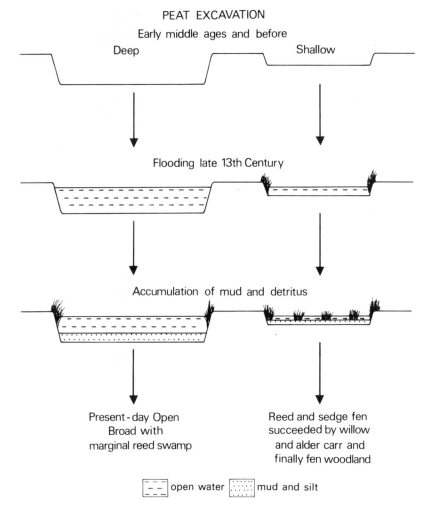

PEAT EXCAVATION
Early middle ages and before

Deep

Shallow

Flooding late 13th Century

Accumulation of mud and detritus

Present-day Open
Broad with
marginal reed swamp

Reed and sedge fen
succeeded by willow
and alder carr and
finally fen woodland

open water   mud and silt

Figure 11. Successional changes following peat excavation in the Broads. For centuries, after flooding, economic use of the marshes, for example reed- and sedge-cutting, coppicing of alder, and grazing by cattle and horses, maintained open conditions and prevented succession to carr and fen woodland.

Today the Norfolk Broads must be regarded as the richest freshwater area surviving in Britain, and it is certainly of international importance for the conservation of marshland and aquatic plants and animals. Two National Nature Reserves have been created, two more have been proposed, and fifteen areas have been notified to the local authorities as

Figure 12. Bure Marshes NNR, Norfolk. This reserve is situated in the heart of the Norfolk Broads and includes over 1000 acres of marshland and open water. The dyke illustrated was originally cut as a route for boating out reed, sedge, and other fen products (see page 32). Today much of the reed bed and grazing marsh is covered with alder/sallow scrub as shown on the left-hand side of this photograph. [*Photo P. Wakeley*]

Sites of Special Scientific Interest. Contained within them are twenty Broads with a total water surface of 1010 acres (420.8 ha).

As the extensive marshlands developed around the Broads, fishing, reed and sedge cutting, and grazing became increasingly important. It seems likely that all these fen products were fully exploited, but shallow peat cutting continued where the water level was not too high. An estate map of the Woodbastwick Marshes (now part of the Bure Marshes NNR [Figure 12]), dated 1845, illustrates the pattern of land use (Figure 13). The greater part of the 500 acres (208 ha) consisted of open fen, either reed and sedge or grazing marsh. In the map for 1845 an extensive shallow peat cutting can be seen in the centre of the marsh, while on the south-western side is the deeper Decoy Broad which, today, still retains

1845

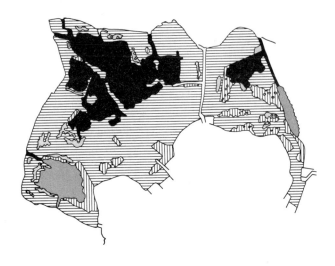

1880

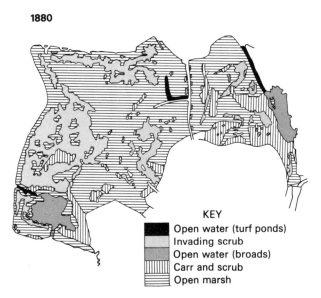

KEY
█ Open water (turf ponds)
▒ Invading scrub
▓ Open water (broads)
▤ Carr and scrub
▤ Open marsh

Figure 13. Vegetation change in the Woodbastwick Marshes from 1845 to 1964. [*The Nature Conservancy, Report on Broadland, 1965*]

1958

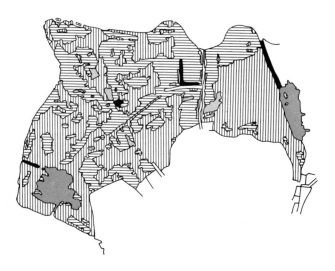

1964

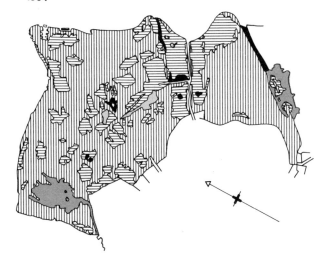

most of its original water surface. By 1880 reedswamp had swept across the shallow excavations and bush growth was beginning to invade the marshes. Eighty years later, in 1969, shrubby fen woodland had spread over most of the area apart from a few small patches where reed or sedge beds had been maintained by regular cutting. As the demand for reed, sedge, and alder coppice declined because of changing economic conditions, and fen litter was no longer required as fodder for horses, natural processes of succession took over, allowing the development from primary fen to a more consolidated herbaceous vegetation, followed by scrub and woodland. This process is of considerable scientific interest in itself but when it extends over most of the marshes as at Woodbastwick, it leads to uniformity and loss of habitat diversity. It is, in fact, the most widespread and difficult management problem in the Broadland nature reserves at the present time[18]. The changing pattern of land use has undoubtedly been the major factor responsible for the marshland landscape differences compared with the last century, but in recent years new activities have developed which may well create additional problems for wildlife conservation.

Today, the open waters of Broadland have become the summer playground of hundreds of thousands of visitors, both from this country and from abroad. Boating holidays on the Broads began to attract the public in the second half of the nineteenth century. One of the early books on the subject (1887) described the peace and solitude of the waters, unbroken even by the commercial sailing wherries[19]. The popularity of the region steadily increased after the turn of the century, especially in the post-war years, when from 1947 to 1964 the annual number of boat licences, of all types, jumped from 3400 to 9247. A Broads Consortium Committee of Local Authorities, River Authority, and the Yarmouth Port and Haven Commissioners has examined this trend, which is maintaining its rate of increase, and predicted that in the year 2000 there could be nearly 20 000 boats on the waterways, made up of 4000 hire cruisers, 1500 day-hire launches, 5800 private sailing dinghies and row-boats, 3500 private motor-boats and 4000 private cruisers and yachts. In addition, angling is becoming increasingly popular so that access to, and maintenance of, the banks of rivers and dykes becomes more important. In 1968, 100 000 fishing licences were granted, an increase of 45 per cent since 1961, and the rate continues to expand at 7 per cent per annum[2].

The total area of water available to meet this growing demand is not very great, although opinions differ on what can be regarded as the 'carrying capacity' of the area—that is, the number of boats which can be tolerated before holiday enjoyment begins to suffer through river traffic congestion. The navigable and accessible Broads have a total water surface of about 900 acres (375 ha); only 4 Broads exceed 100 acres (41.6 ha) in area, and 26 Broads have less than 25 acres (10.4 ha) of water surface. However, the 94 miles (150 km) of navigable rivers (excluding dykes and channels through Broads) have a water area of about 7000 acres (2916 ha) so that in the year 2000, if the total water surface remains unchanged, there will be about $2\frac{1}{2}$ acres (1 ha) for each of the predicted 20 000 boats.

This does not seem to constitute a very high density but, of course, boats are never distributed at random in this way. Already there are areas of great popularity where congestion of river traffic at peak periods may be very high. On some waterways 90 cruisers per hour have been recorded at peak periods and 650 during the course of a day. It is clear that long before the end of the present century a redistribution of boat traffic will be necessary if the pleasure of a boating holiday is to be preserved. Part of the difficulty is that the Broads are distributed unevenly throughout the region. Of the 46 surviving Broads, 34 are situated in the valley of the River Bure and its tributaries, the Ant and the Thurne. It is also in this area that the majority of the Broadland NNRs and SSSIs are found. In addition to the open water some 8000 acres (3333 ha) of unreclaimed marshland, reed and sedge beds remain in the Broadland valleys, most of which occur in the upper reaches of the above three rivers.

The greater part of the total conservation area in the Broads is therefore marshland which does not attract the average tourist, so that the wonderfully rich flora, invertebrate fauna, and birdlife of the marshes are relatively undisturbed by the constant flow of boat traffic on the nearby waterways. On the waters themselves, aquatic birds will tend to avoid the busy routes when feeding, and nests constructed too close to the navigation channels may be swamped by the wash of passing boats. Some ornithologists believe that the failure of that magnificent bird, the marsh harrier, to breed in the Norfolk Broads during the last decade is at least partly due to the level of disturbance, although the decline of this species has been fairly general throughout the country. It has survived best on the relatively small area of marsh at the Minsmere nature reserve, where public access can be carefully controlled.

The concentration of boatyards, other commercial developments for the tourist, and much of the river traffic, in the upper reaches of the

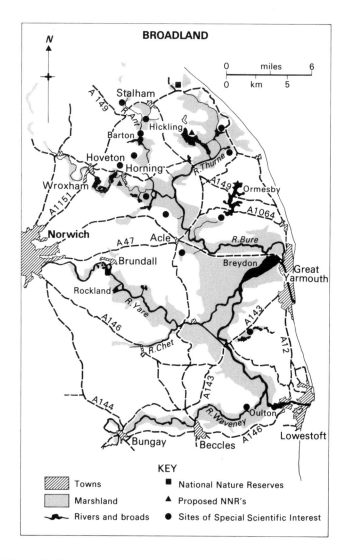

Figure 14. The distribution of National Nature Reserves, proposed NNRs and Sites of Special Scientific Interest in the valleys of the Norfolk Broads. [*After The Nature Conservancy, Report on Broadland, 1965*]

Bure, Ant, and Thurne valleys—the most important wildlife area—may lead to conflict between the two interests in the future (Figure 14). Pressure to gain access to private waters will increase and schemes to dredge out Broads which are overgrown or silted up have been proposed. The case for more open water for recreational purposes is strong, but conservationists and the public who value the unspoilt Broadland landscape would like to see a dispersal of traffic and tourist development by the creation of new waterways in the lower reaches of the river valleys. This would take some of the pressure away from the area of greatest wildlife interest and make better use of the total area of navigable water.

Pollution and eutrophication of the rivers and Broads have increased as the population and tourist industry have expanded. However, the River Authority considers that there is no serious general problem of pollution and that the construction of new treatment plants is keeping pace with the population and demands of industry. Some local problems are recognized: oil discharge from boats, direct discharge of industrial effluents, sewage from holiday craft, and wastes from agriculture such as organic residues, fertilizers, and other chemicals. The greater input of sewage effluent and chemicals of various kinds, although not a health hazard, may have some influence on aquatic vegetation by stimulating the growth of some plants and depressing others. For instance, the impressive floating mats of hornwort (*Ceratophyllum demersum*), which were so characteristic of the Yare Valley Broads ten or more years ago, have now almost entirely disappeared, possibly due to the effluent from Norwich Sewage Works, which discharges upstream[18]. Nevertheless, evidence of such influences is slight and the subject requires a careful and detailed study.

These brief accounts of the Breck and the Broads are only fragments, although important ones, of the wildlife pattern of Britain. It has not been possible to discuss equally important areas, for example, the New Forest, Lake District, Peak District, Snowdonia, the Cairngorms, and many others. But the principles are the same: no wildlife area is 'entire unto itself', and on all sides other activities influence, modify, change, destroy, or, perhaps, sometimes enhance the environment for wildlife. These are facts of modern life but in accepting them we must also try to understand, by research and investigation, how these influences work, whether they can be controlled, and if it is possible to predict the changes which will occur in the future.

The Norfolk Broads and all the other areas listed above, except

Breckland, clearly demonstrate that many areas of high scientific and conservation value also have beautiful landscapes or other features which attract large numbers of the general public. We must accept that man is just as much part of our rural environment as wildlife, and the task of those responsible for conservation research is to explore systems and regimes of management in which neither man nor wildlife loses at the expense of the other. To quote the counsel of Charles Elton, conservation means 'looking for some wise principle of co-existence between man and nature, even if it has to be a modified kind of man and a modified kind of nature'.

4
How is a Nature Reserve Selected?

We have seen in earlier chapters that wildlife conservation cannot be defined entirely in scientific terms. All nature reserves are part of the landscape, contributing to the beauty of the countryside and giving much pleasure to many people who are not specifically interested in plants and animals.

Nevertheless, the Nature Conservancy can only establish an NNR providing the site can be shown to have a scientific value of national importance. Yet in practice other factors must also be considered, for example it may be quite impossible for reasons of ownership, common rights, planning developments, and so on, to obtain control over the best example of a particular type of reserve, but a comparable site of marginally lower scientific status may be offered for purchase, lease or agreement. Therefore, although there are overall rules for assessing scientific status, the basic criteria must be considered in relation to local problems and conditions.

The concept of multipurpose use is widely accepted in Britain for different categories of protected landscapes, but its application to NNRs must always be carefully considered in relation to the type of site and its scientific interest. A large area of chalk down, an extensive moorland, or a wide expanse of open water, can, and often does, act as a focus for tourists without harm to the scientific merit. Fen reserves may serve as washlands in the winter, to absorb flood water from adjacent agricultural land, while on other sites grazing and game preservation may be compatible with conservation. Some reserves, however, have plant and animal communities which are too fragile and vulnerable to disturbance to be able to tolerate public access except of a very limited kind, and perhaps for all nature reserves some degree of control is necessary. The restrictions which must be applied—whether in terms of numbers of visitors, limitation of access to certain seasons of the year, or particular parts of the reserve—will depend on the objects of management and on the type of wildlife communities and the species present.

The criteria for selection

The basis for reserve selection has been comprehensively described in the 1947 White Paper[1]. Its main proposals have not really been changed since then but experience has greatly helped to refine those details which are of greatest value. The White Paper proposed that it was necessary to 'preserve and maintain . . . the main types of community and kinds of wild plants and animals represented in this country, both common and rare, typical and unusual, as well as places which contain physical features of special or outstanding merit'.

This is a splendid statement of intention but presupposes that the fauna and flora of Britain had been adequately studied for the reserves to be selected on a basis of representation. This would not have been possible in 1947 and it was not until twenty years later that the scientific staff of the Nature Conservancy, together with members of the universities and many voluntary conservation bodies, were able to conduct a modern survey of British mountains and moorlands, upland and lowland grasslands, woods, heaths, wetlands including open water, coastlands, and certain artificial habitats. Enormous gaps in our knowledge remain, particularly for the invertebrate fauna, but for the first time it has become possible to make an objective judgement of how well the 135 NNRs are representative of the main types of community and kinds of wild plants and animals in this country. Comparative measurements of scientific value are also needed for proposed nature reserves because, in general, there are more sites than financial resources to acquire them. In other areas, two or more smaller sites, representative of a particular type of interest, may be known and a choice has to be made. For instance, woodlands and heathlands are now fragmented into numerous relatively small units, many of them showing similar characteristics. If a clear choice of a particular site cannot be made on the basis of the available knowledge, it is sometimes advisable to obtain control over an aggregation of small units found in the same general area, usually termed an 'aggregate site'. The scientific case for any *one* of these units may not be very high, but taken as a group they achieve a much higher status.

In addition it is useful to categorize all sites in relation to history and extent of human exploitation. These factors are of special importance for future scientific management. Five categories are used, adapted from the work of Prof. V. Westhoff:

1. *Natural*

In the early days of post-war conservation studies, 'naturalness' was regarded as of outstanding importance and some of the earliest nature reserves were established because they were thought to be relicts of primeval conditions. However, it is generally agreed today that plant and animal communities, unmodified by man or his domestic stock, no longer survive in this country, or, if they do, it is as very small areas on mountain tops, inaccessible rock ledges, some coastlines, salt marshes, and remote water bodies. Such situations, whenever they can be identified with certainty, have considerable scarcity value and consequently high scientific importance. Nevertheless no British nature reserve can be described as wholly natural, although the 60 000 acres (25 000 ha) of the Cairngorms and similar high-altitude areas probably include small components which qualify for this description. Used in this sense, 'natural' formations are completely uninfluenced by man, either directly or indirectly, but 'naturalness' is perhaps a more useful term because it includes some degree of modification while emphasizing natural features.

2. *Near-natural*

These include habitats with a high degree of naturalness and might be described as a spontaneous development of native species in a community very similar to the potential natural ecosystem. Although influenced by man, the natural succession of near-natural formations has not been deflected and no species will have been deliberately introduced or eliminated. Examples include climax forest from which timber and other products have been taken but without causing significant change, and grasslands and moorlands above the tree line, where grazing has taken place. Such areas are scarce in Britain but nevertheless much more widespread than natural habitats, for example certain dunes, shingle banks and salt marshes, some extensive upland and mountain areas, a few raised bogs, and other types of oligotrophic wetland and aquatic systems. Their representation on NNRs, particularly in the north and west of Britain, is therefore better than those of category 1.

3. *Semi-natural*

The term 'semi-natural' is commonly used by conservationists but usually in a very loose sense to describe situations from those which are little modified to others which are almost entirely artificial, but have been allowed to go 'wild'. A satisfactory definition may not be possible but in this account 'semi-natural' formations are assemblages of animals and plants consisting entirely, or predominantly, of native species in ecosystems which have been so modified by man's activities that succession has been completely diverted from its natural course, the existing formation bearing little or no relation to the potential natural ecosystem. Well-known examples are the extensive calcicolous grasslands and heathlands of lowland England, whose climax vegetation would be forest; most woodlands, coppice, scrub, and fenland are also included. A further distinction between this category and the near-natural formation is that in the latter the modification is usually due to a single factor whereas on the majority of semi-natural areas many factors have been responsible for environmental change. This last point characterizes the history of most British nature reserves, so that greater precision in the use of the term 'semi-natural' would be helpful in defining conservation and management problems.

4. Artificial

When the Nature Conservancy was created in 1949, man-made wildlife areas were not thought to be of importance to the nature reserve system. Today, with a much better knowledge of the distribution of plants and animals, it is known that such sites may be important wildlife refuges. In a densely populated industrial country such as Britain, examples of these habitats are diverse and widespread and include disused gravel, clay and chalk pits and quarries, abandoned railway tracks, banks and verges of road and rail cuttings, canals, reservoirs, land flooded by mining subsidence, spoil tips and so on.

5. Agricultural

This category should be included because some types of land in agricultural use, for example permanent pasture and other grasslands not ploughed for a very long time, are well represented on many nature reserves and other categories of protected areas. Such grasslands, however, would normally be regarded as semi-natural in this classification. The other components of the farm landscape, such as crops, sown leys, orchards, ponds, plantations and hedgerows, also make an important contribution to conservation, because in total they cover such a large area. Nevertheless they are normally not found within sites managed primarily for wildlife.

We can now turn our attention to other criteria which are relevant to all sites in the above classification, although their importance varies according to the ecological characteristics of the reserves and certain local conditions such as history, management and nearness of comparable sites.

Diversity

The richness of the flora and fauna of a reserve is determined by many biotic and physical features of the environment. Differences in local climate, topography, water regime, aspect, soils, and altitude, all influence the range of variation in the vegetation cover and occurrence of plant species, and consequently the diversity of habitats for animal life. Such natural differences will be generally more obvious on large rather than small areas, as illustrated in the totals of plant species recorded by van der Maarel in plots of different sizes on a Dutch dune system[20].

Species	Area (m^2)	Site
30	$\frac{1}{16}$	Dune slack
40	2	Dune slack and grassland
70	10	Dwarf scrub on dune
90	200	Mature dune scrub
130	2 000	Sandy grass heath
220	10 000 (1 ha or 2.4 acres)	Dune grassland

Some nature reserves of modest size may be particularly rich in habitat variety, for example Cavenham Heath NNR (337 acres, 140.4 ha) in West Suffolk, which includes within a short distance a zonation of woodland, scrub, heath, grassland, fen, and open water. In this, and many other semi-natural areas, the present-day vegetational and habitat diversity is mainly a direct result of past human activities. It leads, very often, to a condition of ecological instability so that continued management is necessary to prevent undesirable changes. The rich flora of chalk downs is maintained by grazing, that of a water meadow by mowing; a heath managed by rotational burning has greater variety than one which is not burned; and a fen which is cropped for reed, sedge, and litter is richer in species than a similar area where succession to carr has taken place. This type of 'man-induced' biological diversity must be distinguished from that in natural or near-natural ecosystems such as tropical rain forest, where complexity, as expressed in numbers of species and potential niches, is believed to create ecological stability.

It is generally easier to measure diversity in terms of species or communities of plants because they can be readily identified and mapped. In addition they are often regarded as a reliable index of richness of animal communities and species. The latter point is usually a valid assumption because many animals feed on plants and are often host-specific. At the same time, different growth-forms of plants create different micro-environments and increase the range of ecological niches. This introduces a new factor of great importance to invertebrate animals—habitat structure, a component which is not necessarily related to floristic richness. Ungrazed grassland usually has fewer plant species than the same vegetation which is grazed, but the animal life of the former will be richer in numbers and species. This is because in ungrazed grassland a litter layer forms over the ground, the herbs produce more leaves and are able to flower and fruit, increasing the range of exploitable material for invertebrate life. A woodland with a varied structure of old and young trees, mature and new coppice, glades and rides, will be richer zoologically than a more uniform woodland with the same plant species. Decomposing organic material, such as leaf litter, dead and dying wood, also has a rich fauna, and so adds to zoological diversity, although not influenced by floristic richness. It is important to recognize this distinction, particularly in nature reserve management, because the botanical and zoological objectives concerning biological diversity may have to be achieved by different means. A further expression of habitat structure can be seen in the type of margin which develops or is maintained around major vegetation formations. This is termed the 'edge effect' and may consist of an abrupt change from one type of vegetation to another (an ecotone) or a gradual zonation (an ecocline). The significance of these will be discussed more fully when we consider animal habitats.

In summary we can say that ecological diversity, as expressed in numbers of species, communities, and habitats, is probably the most important criterion in the selection of nature reserves. However, it is necessary to distinguish between natural diversity, that is the intrinsic characteristics of the site, both physical and biological, and the type of biological diversity brought about by man's activities. The latter may be of considerable importance where traditional forms of land use have been established for a very long period, but in other cases artificially created diversity is usually transient and unstable.

A large number of indices for the measurement of diversity have been devised by statisticians; for an introduction to those most commonly used, the reader should consult *Ecological Methods* by T. R. E. Southwood[21].

Rarity

Great importance is usually attached to this criterion because many rare species of plants and animals have great appeal for most naturalists and the general public with an interest in nature. Professional ecologists apply this term to ecosystems, communities, and habitats as well as to species, and the scientific reasons for conserving the first three are often considered to be of greater importance, whether or not they support rare plants and animals. However, if the nature reserve system is to be truly representative, then we must attempt to give equal consideration to all the different aspects of rarity in nature.

The reasons for species rarity are not well understood. An animal or plant may be on the edge of its climatic range and vulnerable to small environmental changes; some have a very discontinuous distribution and apparently occur as relicts of what was once a more widespread population; while other species have very specialized habitat requirements and become rare when the habitat is rare. In addition there are numerous species which are rare for no obvious reason, as in the case of some insects which feed on common foodplants, for example the black hairstreak butterfly which feeds on blackthorn. Some plants, such as the pasque flower, the snakeshead, and several orchids of calcareous soils, are also much scarcer than the habitat conditions in which they grow (Figure 15).

A number of larger animals, the polecat, pine marten, wildcat, golden eagle, and kite, which became rare as a result of persistent persecution by man, recovered when landowners were persuaded to tolerate them or they were protected by law. Protection, particularly of breeding sites, has enabled species like the black-tailed godwit, ruff, avocet, bittern, osprey, and marsh harrier, to re-establish as breeding birds after the original British populations had become extinct. Perhaps the main factor contributing to rarity during the last thirty to forty years is the destruction or modification of wildlife habitats due to urban spread and progress in agricultural technology. This trend started with the beginning

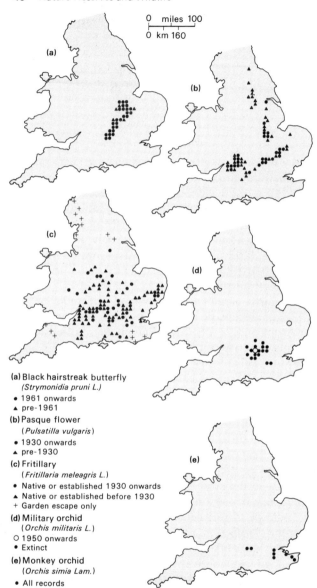

(a) Black hairstreak butterfly
   (Strymonidia pruni L.)
   ● 1961 onwards
   ▲ pre-1961
(b) Pasque flower
   (*Pulsatilla vulgaris*)
   ● 1930 onwards
   ▲ pre-1930
(c) Fritillary
   (*Fritillaria meleagris L.*)
   ● Native or established 1930 onwards
   ▲ Native or established before 1930
   + Garden escape only
(d) Military orchid
   (*Orchis militaris L.*)
   ○ 1950 onwards
   ● Extinct
(e) Monkey orchid
   (*Orchis simia Lam.*)
   ● All records

Figure 15. Distribution maps of the (a) black hairstreak butterfly, (b) pasque flower, (c) fritillary (snakeshead), (d) military orchid, and (e) monkey orchid, in the British Isles. [*From the Biological Records Centre of the Nature Conservancy*]

of the Industrial Revolution, but accelerated greatly during and after the Second World War. Drainage, afforestation, destruction of hedgerows, ploughing, widespread use of herbicides and insecticides, increasing use of fertilizers, industrial pollution, and tourist development in rural areas, have all taken their toll.

One of the best illustrations of this can be obtained by an analysis of the very comprehensive data on plants assembled for the Atlas of the British Flora[22] and in the years following its publication in 1962 by the Biological Records Centre at the Monks Wood Experimental Station. Rarity was defined as the occurrence in fifteen or less 10-km squares out of a total of 2750 in Great Britain. Two hundred and seventy-eight species fell into this category. In 1950 these species were recorded from 1902 localities and 10 years later this had fallen to 1425 localities, a decrease of 25 per cent. In the period 1600 to 1900 only 7 species are known to have become extinct, but from 1900 to 1970 a further 13 have been lost. In addition more and more species are entering the category of 'very rare', that is, those restricted to one or two 10-km squares. Before 1900 there were only 44 such species; in 1930 there were 59; and in 1970 the figure had risen to 97[23]. Although rarity may be due to several natural causes, there is no doubt that the recent rapid acceleration of this trend is mainly a consequence of man's activities. In Table 2, 26 out of 34 rare plants are shown which have declined for reasons associated with farming, land management, and collecting activities. A good example is the snakeshead (*Fritillaria meleagris*), a rare plant of 'unimproved' hay meadows, which soon disappears if management is changed to grazing by cattle or sheep so that seed formation is prevented. The three distribution maps in Figure 16 show the decline of this species during the last forty to fifty years.

These comprehensive data enable us to assess the representation of flowering plants on conservation areas. The three categories of *Very Rare* (1−2 10-km squares), *Rare* (3−15 10-km squares), and *Very Local* (16−100 10-km squares) include a total of 552 species, of which 82.8 per cent occur on existing or proposed nature reserves. Available information on the British fauna is nothing like so comprehensive, with the possible exception of British butterflies. Of 13 rare species (defined in this case by occurrence in 6 or less 10-km squares), all but 2 are represented on existing or proposed nature reserves, while 18 out of 92 rare moths are absent from such sites. In these two groups the proportion which receives, or is likely to receive, protection, is relatively high, and the same appears to be the case for dragonflies, weevils and spiders, although the survey data are less complete.

Table 2. Decline in the status of 34 very rare plants from 1900 to 1960. Numbers refer to the 10 km squares occupied. [Perring[23]]

Probable cause	Squares 1900	1930	1960	Localities 1900	1950	1960
Changes in arable farming						
Anthoxanthum puelii	62	9	2	69	9	2
Bromus interruptus	21	11	1	76	1	1
Lythrum hyssopifolia	37	5	1	51	3	2
Polycarpon tetraphyllum	14	5	2	15	6	6
Rhinanthus serotinus	71	10	2	83	6	2
Veronica triphyllos	23	5	2	29	5	3
V. verna	8	3	2	8	3	2
Ploughing						
Armeria elongata	6	2	1	6	2	1
Artemisia campestris	11	12	2	15	3	2
Eryngium campestre	22	12	2	33	6	2
Gnaphalium luteo-album	6	4	1	7	4	2
Juncus capitatus	8	4	1	9	2	1
Scorzonera humilis	3	3	1	3	2	1
Drainage						
Galium debile	5	5	2	7	5	3
Liparis loeselii	27	12	2	38	11	2
Scheuchzeria palustris	9	3	1	9	1	1
Selinum carvifolia	5	3	2	5	3	2
Viola stagnina	15	7	2	21	3	3
Collecting						
Cyclamen hederifolium	4	2	1	6	2	1
Cypripedium calceolus	19	3	1	24	1	1
Gentiana nivalis	4	3	2	4	3	2
Lychnis alpina	3	3	2	5	3	2
Minuartia rubella	5	3	2	6	3	2
Scrub and woodland management						
Carex depauperata	6	3	2	8	2	2
Euphorbia corallioides	4	4	1	4	2	1
Lack of management						
Ranunculus ophioglossifolius	4	3	1	4	3	2
Natural causes						
Crepis foetida	16	4	1	24	3	2
Elatine hydropiper	9	4	2	16	4	2
Matthiola incana	4	4	1	6	2	1
M. sinuata	16	1	1	18	2	1
Orchis militaris	18	1	2	29	2	2
O. simia	8	3	2	11	5	3
Orobanche picridis	22	5	1	24	3	1
Spartina alterniflora	4	1	1	4	1	1

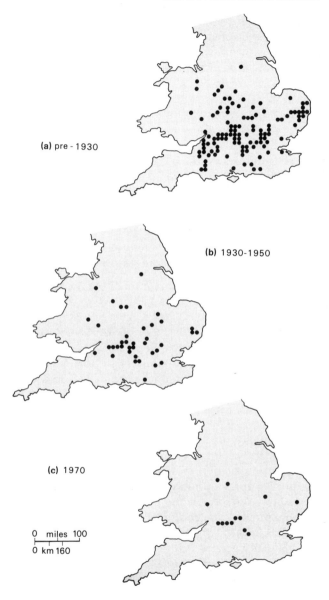

Figure 16. The decline of the snakeshead (*Fritillaria meleagris*) in England, from 1930-1970. [*From data compiled by D. A. Wells*]

It is clear that the overriding factor creating rarity in both plants and animals is the loss of habitat and environmental conditions necessary for survival, particularly of the more specialized species. This emphasizes the need for representation of high natural diversity in our system of nature reserves.

Although we usually assess rarity only in terms of British conditions, there is sometimes a good case for taking a broader view by considering the European status and distribution of a species. For example, the bluebell is a common and widespread woodland plant in this country, while elsewhere it is restricted to the northern parts of France and Belgium and the French Atlantic coast. But there is no doubt that the finest bluebell woods occur in this country. Conversely the pasque flower, which is now very scarce in southern England, has a wide distribution in Europe and is not an endangered species.

Size, shape, and surrounding of nature reserves

On pages 26-27 examples have been given of the fragmentation of former extensive heathland in Dorset and the East Anglian Breckland into many small areas, often isolated from each other by agricultural land or plantations. On theoretical grounds a small isolated unit is likely to be less varied biologically than a larger area, and its wildlife will be more vulnerable to disturbance or destruction from outside influences. In addition, local extinction of species is more likely to occur, either by accident or as a result of natural fluctuations in a small population, and the chance of re-establishment by dispersal from elsewhere is reduced. Experimental evidence for these hypotheses is very scarce, but the Dorset heaths studied produced some information that isolation may lead to an impoverishment of the fauna (Figure 17).

In this case the units were fairly large, averaging about 67 acres (27.9 ha) in area, and a separation of 5 km or more from the main heath areas seemed to be effective in preventing colonization by certain species of birds and reptiles. A comparison of the herbaceous flora of two large woodland areas fragmented into units 0.8 km apart in one case and 0.4 km in another suggested that 0.8 km might be a critical distance, beyond which the successful dispersal of certain plants to similar areas might be greatly reduced[24]. However, in the former case the woodland units had been separated since the thirteenth century so that dispersal had been able to act over a long period, while in the latter case the woods were practically contiguous until the eighteenth century. Time,

Figure 17. The effects of isolation on the distribution of eight heathland indicator animals in 1960. The numerals show the number of species observed in the area indicated. In each case the numeral above the line refers to species confined to heathland habitats, the lower figure to species which are found in other habitats as well. [*Moore*[17]]

and distance from the nearest similar site, are therefore both important factors in assessing the effects of isolation.

Small colonies of perennial plants are sometimes remarkably persistent. Tamm in Sweden has suggested that the half life (the time taken for half the population to die out) of a colony of cowslips may be at least fifty years[25]. Seeds of many plants may also remain viable in the soil for a very long period. Two common annual weeds, *Chenopodium album* and *Spergularia arvensis,* have been recorded on archaeological evidence as retaining their viability for 1700 years[26]. On Woodwalton Fen NNR the very rare fen violet *Viola stagnina* appeared in large numbers in a cleared area which had been covered with hawthorn scrub for about forty years (Figure 18). The scrub was so thick that virtually all the ground vegetation had been suppressed for some time, but in the first season after clearance large numbers of the violet appeared and flowered.

The size of a reserve cannot always be measured in terms of area. A detailed study by L. K. Ward on the distribution of juniper and its fauna has shown that an isolated population of 100 bushes or less, more than

Figure 18. The fen violet (*Viola stagnina*) growing on recently cleared ground on Woodwalton Fen.

2 miles (3.2 km) from the nearest similar colony, is likely to have fewer of the 16 specialized juniper insects than a similar area close to other juniper populations. The age of the bushes is also important because several of the rarer specialist insect species feed on the fruit of juniper which is not produced until the bush is several years old. In addition this plant is dioecious so that on an average one can only expect half the population to produce fruit.

In general, the larger the vertebrate animal the greater the area needed to sustain a viable population, but a distinction must be made between herbivores and predators. High numbers of the former may occur in areas of food abundance, for example in the Uganda National Park elephants were recorded at 8.7 to the square mile (2.6 km^2) in a wooded savanna region[27], and in North America 125 white-tailed deer to the square mile could be tolerated without the habitat showing signs of overgrazing. On the other hand a pair of golden eagles may need 28 square miles

(73.7 km^2) or more in Scotland as hunting territory. Tawny owls require from 10 to 30 acres (4.2 to 12.5 ha), depending on density of rodent population, and the red-backed shrike, which feeds mainly on insects but which also takes small birds, has a recorded territory size varying from 1.4 to 8.3 acres (0.58 to 3.4 ha). The Minsmere marshland nature reserve of the Royal Society for the Protection of Birds (1500 acres, 625 ha) and the Hickling Broad National Nature Reserve (1204 acres (501.6 ha) including 300 acres (125 ha) of open water) have never been able to sustain more than 5 pairs of breeding marsh harriers, and it is certain that at these densities the birds range widely outside the reserve boundaries when hunting. A recent study of a wolf pack in Canada containing 8 individuals showed that, over a period of 46 days, the pack ranged over an area of 124.2 square miles (327 km^2) and covered on an average 4.4 miles (7.1 km) per day.

For invertebrate predators much smaller areas may be sufficient. On a Danish heath it was found that the rare burrow-living spider *Eresus niger* had established what appeared to be a thriving colony on a sandy heathland verge 2 to 3 yards (72-108 cm) wide situated between a road and a conifer plantation. Similarly the rare linyphiid spider *Acanthophyma gowerensis* seems to be confined to a narrow zone only a few metres wide, on the upper part of certain salt-marshes[28]. Some specialized plant-feeding insects may also maintain themselves in relatively small areas where the foodplant occurs, for example in a fungus on rotting wood.

In general for reserves which are modest in size, say 50 acres (20.7 ha) or less, the nearer the shape is to a circle or square, so that the peripheral zone is at a minimum, the less will be the effect of disturbance from activities on adjacent land. Spray drift from agricultural land may not penetrate so far, and fewer breeding birds will be disturbed by external noise. Immigration of undesirable plants will also be slower, for example invasion of grass or heath by scrub. An assessment of how near the shape of a reserve is to the 'ideal' can be made by calculating the perimeter ratio,

$$p = \frac{\text{length of perimeter of reserve}}{\text{length of perimeter of same area in circular form}}$$

The nearer this value is to 1, the closer is the shape to the supposed ideal. There are many exceptions to this general rule, however, because smaller reserves may consist of transition zones from one vegetation type to another—a scarp slope too steep to plough, a roadside verge and hedge or bank of an abandoned railway, a canal, a dune ridge, or cliff edge. The shape of the reserve therefore depends on the particular scientific feature which must be maintained.

Reserves close to urban areas or situated in an agricultural region often benefit by the creation of a surrounding *buffer zone* in which certain activities are restricted. Control of drainage water flowing into a reserve surrounded by agricultural land may be vital to the maintenance of the appropriate water regime, and shooting rights may have to be acquired on land around a reserve with high ornithological interest.

In this chapter we have considered in some detail the main factors influencing the selection of nature reserves, particularly those of national importance. The scientific reasons offered in support of candidate areas are rarely comprehensive biologically, and in a number of cases similar sites of comparable status may compete for the limited financial resources. Selection may therefore have to be decided in some instances by an assessment of the importance of small ecological differences or for non-scientific reasons, such as access control, position or size. In all cases, however, the special scientific features claimed for the site should be considered in relation to measurements of ecological diversity, particularly richness of species and communities, together with a record of the potential animal habitats derived from the Animal Habitat Chart of the Nature Conservancy's Management Plan for nature reserves. In addition, available information on land-use history will help us to evaluate past human modifications and the degree of naturalness. We should then examine the problems of survival and maintenance of the species, communities and habitats in the context of the shape, size, and surroundings of the site including a potential buffer zone. Finally, it is important to remember that the reliability of our decisions in relation to these criteria depends, very largely, on the extent and quality of our knowledge of the plants and animals themselves, particularly their biology, ecology, and distribution.

5
What is a Habitat?

A few years ago the term 'habitat' was familiar only to scientists and naturalists, but today the environment-conscious public has taken it into everyday use almost as commonly as the word 'ecology'. Inevitably its meaning has become more diffuse and many scientists think that it should now be replaced by the term 'biotope', which is well known in scientific literature and means the same thing, that is, the living place and environment in which an organism is found. However, 'habitat' is so widely used that it is not likely to be abandoned, although in the context of conservation ecology we should make clear precisely what we mean when we use it in connection with scientific work. Closely related to 'habitat' and 'biotope' is the term 'niche', which describes the function and status of an organism within a community. Hutchinson has succinctly illustrated the difference by describing 'habitat' as a 'percept' and 'niche' as a 'concept', while Odum has called the 'habitat' of an organism its 'address' and the niche its 'profession'. But perhaps the best description of a niche is the charming analogy used by Charles Elton, who said that when a naturalist exclaims 'There goes the badger', he should have a picture in his mind of its function and status in the animal community, comparable to his knowledge of human society when he says 'there goes the vicar'.

Although the difference in meaning between habitat and niche is clear, it is impossible to discuss one without frequent reference to the other, because organisms in nature rarely if ever occur as isolated single-species populations in contact only with the physical environment. They are influenced at every stage of their life cycle by the activities of other organisms, so that biotic factors, such as competition, predation, parasitism, and availability of food, may determine whether or not a species is present in a particular habitat—the 'address', in fact, may sometimes already be overcrowded, or else the occupants unfriendly.

So far the definitions referred to imply that a habitat is an area of space, has shape and physical presence, dimensions and boundaries, so that it can be measured and quantified. This is a useful concept because a conservationist responsible for selecting and managing nature reserves could apply it to practical problems without much difficulty. By incorporating a larger number of shapes and structural dimensions, in terms of floristics and vegetation types on nature reserves, the biological diversity would be increased. If we could then predict which species of animals and plants would be associated with these habitats, reserve management would be a comparatively straightforward procedure. Unfortunately the real-life situation is not as simple as this. Macfadyen has pointed out that the habitat of an animal species will vary from place to place according to geographical location, and that it will also be influenced by season, seral succession, and predominance of other species[29]. Immature stages of animals often have different habitats from the adults, and both may vary according to environmental circumstances which are constantly changing in time. For these reasons it is difficult, except in a generalized way, to refer to a particular habitat as being 'typical' of a named species.

Most of the scientific literature dealing with habitats is zoological and the term seems to be of less value to the botanist. Part of the reason is that in plants the species concept is more difficult to define because of the greater range of variation in many taxa, and populations frequently include hybrids and ecotypes. In some dioecious plants the geographical distribution of the female is different from that of the male (as in the butterbur *Petasites hybridus*), ecoclines in relation to environmental gradients are more marked than in animal populations, and other factors, such as differences in soil chemistry within the same habitat, may be responsible for morphological and physiological variations in a population occupying a small area. Tansley, in his classic work, *The British Isles and their vegetation*[30], writes: 'In the study of vegetation the term habitat is applied to the whole complex of environmental factors which differentiate units of vegetation, and is not used in the limited sense of a particular soil or situation'. In the rest of this chapter, habitats will be discussed almost entirely in relation to the fauna.

Describing the animal habitat

There are two main approaches to this problem. A label can be assigned to a particular species, describing its habitat preferences, or else a system of classification of habitats can be adopted and the animal community of each component studied. Both are important but have their limitations as well as values. In the first case, perhaps the most straightforward situation is illustrated by an invertebrate species which feeds only on a single species of plant. Strict monophagy is rather rare in relation to the total fauna of Britain, but examples can be found in a number of different groups, as, for example, some leaf-mining Lepidoptera and gall midges. Some parasitic insects are also very host-specific. Nevertheless, although we know from this information that a certain species will be absent from a site if a particular foodplant or host is not present, it does not help us to explain why that species is not found on numerous other occasions, when its food plant is present in abundance. There are many examples of this sort of situation; the black hairstreak butterfly, whose larvae feed on blackthorn, and the large copper butterfly, whose larvae feed on great water dock, have been mentioned elsewhere. They are both rare insects and yet linked to a common food plant.

It is more usual, however, for phytophagous insects to feed on a range of different plant species, although preferences may be shown for a particular species, genus or family. Predatory invertebrates are generally not so specific in choice of food, although the range of prey species taken may be limited because the predator's activities are restricted to a particular habitat. In fact the physical components of the environment— shelter, light, shade, temperature, dryness or humidity—may be more important, in some instances, in determining the range of movements of the predator than the need to search for a particular prey. These physical characteristics of the environment have been widely used to describe the place or 'address' of an animal in a particular ecosystem. Tretzel[31], in Germany, made an extensive study of 350 species of spiders, based on 34 000 specimens, trapped along a transect which passed through different types of grassland, scrub, and woodland. For each species taken in sufficient numbers, he was able to list those situations in which it occurred and those from which it was absent, and from the relative numbers taken in different places he assigned the species to a 'centre of distribution' or 'optimal' habitat. Tretzel then defined a system of habitat characteristics based on structural components of height and size, together with gradations of light, shade, and moisture.

Height Zones
   A   under stones, and in earth fissures
   B   litter layer

C herb layer 5-50 cm
D bushes, 50-150 cm
E trees, 1.5-4.0 m
F parts of trees above 4.0 m

Light Zones

Increasing moisture
  1. Photobiont—xerobiont
  2. Photobiont—hygrobiont   to each of these
  3. Photobiont—hydrobiont   categories a vertical
Increasing shade and moisture   stratum can be
  4. Hemi-ombrobiont/hemi-hygrobiont   applied, A-F
  5. Hemi-ombrobiont/hygrobiont
  6. Ombrobiont—hygrobiont

A specialized species which could only be assigned to one height zone and one light/moisture category would be described as having a stenoecious ecological valency, while a species occurring in a wide range of categories would be euryoecious. This method of categorizing species according to physical features of the environment has been widely used on the continent and presumably found to be of value. It has certain disadvantages, however. It ignores the presence of biotic factors which influence the occurrence of a species in a particular habitat, but perhaps this is not a real criticism because no-one has yet found a method of assessing the influence of these factors. On the other hand species are assigned to the environmental categories by a subjective process because measurements of light and moisture are not usually made. Perhaps the chief limitation is that the system assumes that the ecology of a species does not change from one part of its geographical range to another, so that the ecological description really only applies to the situation in the area where it has been studied. In another part of its geographical range a different 'label' would probably have to be used.

The other method of habitat description was devised by Charles Elton for the Wytham Ecological Survey. This study, which Mr Elton directed for over fifteen years, analysed the fauna of 1000 acres (416.6 ha) of woodland, scrub, marsh, and meadow, in relation to structural components of the environment. Elton argued that ecologists should accept the fact that ecosystems are very complex situations, and his habitat classification system was an attempt to provide a framework of units which would serve as a basis for more intensive and precise studies of animal communities, niches, habitats, and species inter-relationships.

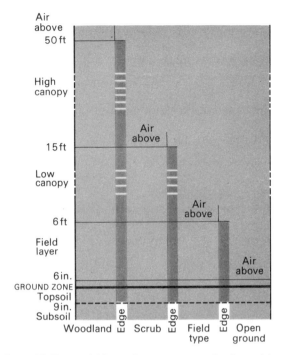

Figure 19. Terrestrial formation types and their edges, with stratification of vertical layers. Field Type includes rotation arable, and Open Ground includes close-grazed pasture. [*C. S. Elton*[10]]

The classification uses six Habitat Systems divided into Formation Types, which could be further subdivided by the use of terms called 'Qualifiers'. These Systems include everything between low-tide mark on the coast and the uppermost free-living animals in the atmosphere. They are: *terrestrial; aquatic; aquatic/terrestrial transition; subterranean* (caves and underground water); *domestic* (buildings, gardens, and other man-made structures); and *general* (dead and dying wood, macrofungi, dung, carrion, animal artefacts such as nests and burrows, and human artefacts such as fence posts, stacks, spoil heaps). The most important of these to the conservationist are the first three, which can be applied to almost all nature reserves including coastal sites which are designated to the main Systems by the use of Qualifiers. The Formation Types are best understood by reference to Figure 19 and are applied to the Terrestrial and Aquatic/Terrestrial Transition Systems.

Formation types
Open ground type: Bare soil, rock and vegetation not more than 6 in. (15 cm) in height in open situations. It includes grazed grassland, heaths, and other open areas from dunes to arctic-alpine regions above the treeline.

Field type: Open habitats such as tall grassland, heather, marram dunes, low scrub, and fen vegetation, over 6 in. (15 cm) in height and not exceeding 6 ft (2 m).

Scrub type: Bushes and young trees over 6 ft (2 m) but not exceeding 15 ft (4.5 m) in height.

Woodland type: Tree canopy exceeding 15 ft in height.

Vertical zones are distinguished for each Formation Type. In the woodland Formation Type the zones include Subsoil and Rock, Topsoil, Ground Zone (all low-growing vegetation and other ground features less than 6 in. (15 cm) in height), Field Layer (herbs and shrubs not exceeding 6 ft (2 m) but excluding the lower 6 in. which would be part of the Ground Zone), Low Canopy or Scrub Zone (vegetation between 6 ft and 15 ft (4.5 m)), and High Canopy (parts of trees over 15 ft).

The Qualifiers are particularly important because we can then subdivide the Open Ground and Field Types, in terms of soil and vegetation, into Acid, Non-acid, Maritime, and Arable. The Maritime Qualifier includes drier mudbanks, sand dunes, shingle spits, and sea cliffs, but not the areas immediately above or between the tide marks, which belong to the Transition System. The Qualifiers used for Scrub and Woodland are Deciduous, Conifer, and Mixed. Where a few conifers are found in a broad-leaved woodland, the site is designated according to the dominant form. One of the most important parts of a Woodland, Scrubland, or in some cases the Field Zone, is the 'Edge', where it merges into the adjacent, i.e. lower, formation. A Woodland Edge, for instance, although usually a narrow transition zone, is often richer in species of animals than the heart of the woodland under a closed canopy. The Scrub/Field Type Edge, and the Field Type/Open Ground Type Edge may also include mosaics of each habitat which shelter species from both of the main formations.

The Aquatic System is based on speed of flow and size of water body, as illustrated in Table 3. The water bodies vary in size from puddles or tree holes to large lakes, and from still water to waterfalls and torrents. Qualifiers categorize water bodies as Freshwater, Brackish, or Saline, and the vertical layers are Bottom, Water Mass, Submerged Vegetation, Water

Table 3. Water bodies classified by size and speed. [C. S. Elton[10]]

	A Very Small	B Small	C Medium	D Large	E Very Large
1. Still	Tree-hole	Small pond <20 sq yd (17 m²)	Pond <1 acre (0.4 ha)	Large pool or tarn <100 acres (40 ha)	Lake or sea
2. Slow	Trickle, shallow stream	Ditch, field dyke	Canal, river back-water		
3. Medium	Trickle, shallow stream	Lowland brook or small stream	Lowland river	Lowland large river	River estuary
4. Fast	Spring	Upland small torrent stream	Large torrent stream		
5. Vertical or steep	Water drip, pipe outlet, cascade	Small weir or waterfall	Large weir or medium waterfall	Large waterfall	

Surface, Emergent Vegetation, and Air Above. The first two can be further subdivided into Light or Dark.

The Aquatic/Terrestrial Transition System, in addition to the margins of freshwater bodies, includes saltmarshes and the intertidal zone of the seashore. In size a Transition area may vary from a narrow strip of vegetation fringing a water body, to extensive marshes. It is characterized by one or more of the following features: waterlogged ground, fluctuations in water supply, and proximity to a water body. Transition habitats are identified by the formation type of water body they adjoin, although the terrestrial components are recorded as well. Vertical layers in this System conform to those of the Terrestrial habitat, while the Qualifiers are the subsoil categories already mentioned, together with 'Brackish' and 'Saline'.

This very brief outline of the Wytham Habitat Classification can only mention some of the facets to this approach to a very complex problem, but the reader is advised to consult Mr Elton's *The Pattern of Animal Communities* where the philosophy and methodology are described with great clarity[10]. The original purpose of the classification, which was linked with a comprehensive Species Recording Card, was to provide a tool for the study of the structure and organization of animal communities, and it was not until a later stage that its value in conservation work was recognized. It was adopted by the Nature Conservancy to form a 'Chart' of Animal Habitats, each category being represented by a 'box' in which one could write notes describing the vegetation and other features. The purpose of the Chart was to enable the surveyor to make an assessment of the habitat diversity of a site, in relation to its potential faunistic richness. Comparison could then be made between ecologically similar sites. The completed chart is attached to the Reserve Management Plan and provides a basis for the account on the fauna.

The Wytham method was also incorporated in a different type of recording scheme devised by the Society for the Promotion of Nature Reserves to report on and assess the interest of sites which are potential nature reserves[32]. This scheme combines structural components with defined vegetation types of which woodland can be qualified by the names of fifteen common tree species. Three hierarchical levels are described. The first consists of twelve major habitats each denoted by a capital letter symbol: Woodland (F), Scrub (S), Dwarf Scrub (D), Tall Herb (T), Reed Bed (P), Grassland and Short Herbs (G), Moss Communities (B), Open Habitats (O), River (R), Lake (L), Arable (A), and Edge (E). Habitats F, S, D, T, and G have height zones assigned to them, although these are different from the Eltonian system. The Open habitats are defined as areas where the total vegetation cover is less than about 25 per cent. Reed beds and moss communities are considered to be important enough for major habitat ranking. The second and third levels of the hierarchical system consist of symbols which qualify the major habitats in various ways. The habitat data are combined on the same card with general information about the site, such as locality, grid reference, county, vice-county number, Conservancy region, date, geology, altitude, acreage, status (whether a nature reserve, common land, or private, etc.), land use, special scientific interest, owner, tenant, name of surveyor, and other remarks (Figure 20).

A species card is also used with this classification. Standard 5 × 8 in. (12.5 × 20 cm) cards carry a complete list of species of a particular group, for example, vascular plants, spiders, or birds. The recorder draws a line through the names of those species recorded, and in the case of the bryophytes, lichens and invertebrate species cards, there is space to enter a frequency symbol and a microhabitat symbol, the latter forming part of a fourth level in the hierarchy.

This scheme, like the others described, has advantages and

disadvantages depending on the particular interest of the surveyor. Many non-professional naturalists think that they are complicated and difficult to understand or follow. One must remember, however, that they are attempting to make a simple, orderly arrangement out of a very complex situation, in which boundaries between habitats are often diffuse, structural components change with season and succession, water regimes alter with climate, and formations are often modified by human activities. The newcomer to habitat classification may find it easier, in the first place, to think in terms of the three major divisions suggested by Schaeffer[33]. Different types of landscapes are called the *macro-pattern;* physiognomically definable regions (major vegetation formations) form the *meso-pattern,* while small habitat units such as tussocks, holes, dead wood, etc., make up the *micro-pattern* or micro-spatial system. Following on from this there should be no difficulty in using the Habitat Chart because the different categories are illustrated in diagrammatic form. And then, with practice, comparatively little time will be needed to become familiar with the full procedure of either the Eltonian or SPNR systems.

The ecological significance of structure

The choice by Elton and other ecologists of structural units to designate habitats was based partly on convenience, because this was the easiest way of simplifying the complexity of nature, and partly on the recognition of its ecological importance. As an example of the latter, let us consider adjacent areas of grazed and ungrazed grasslands on the same soil type. In phytosociological terms the two areas of vegetation would not be distinguished as separate communities, but a study of the invertebrate faunas would show considerable differences. Grassland which has been regularly grazed by sheep for a number of years will average perhaps only two or three inches (5-7.5 cm) in height, or even less if the grazing has been intense. In addition, trampling and exposure to sun and wind tends to fragment and disperse the small accumulations of leaf litter and dry out the soil surface.

In the absence of grazing and trampling, grasses and other herbs grow taller and are able to flower and fruit, and a litter of dead plant material begins to form. On a chalk grassland which had not been grazed or trampled for seven years, 73.7 per cent dry weight of the total plant material consisted of litter[34]. The erect plants shade and protect the litter from desiccation and this in turn maintains equable conditions over

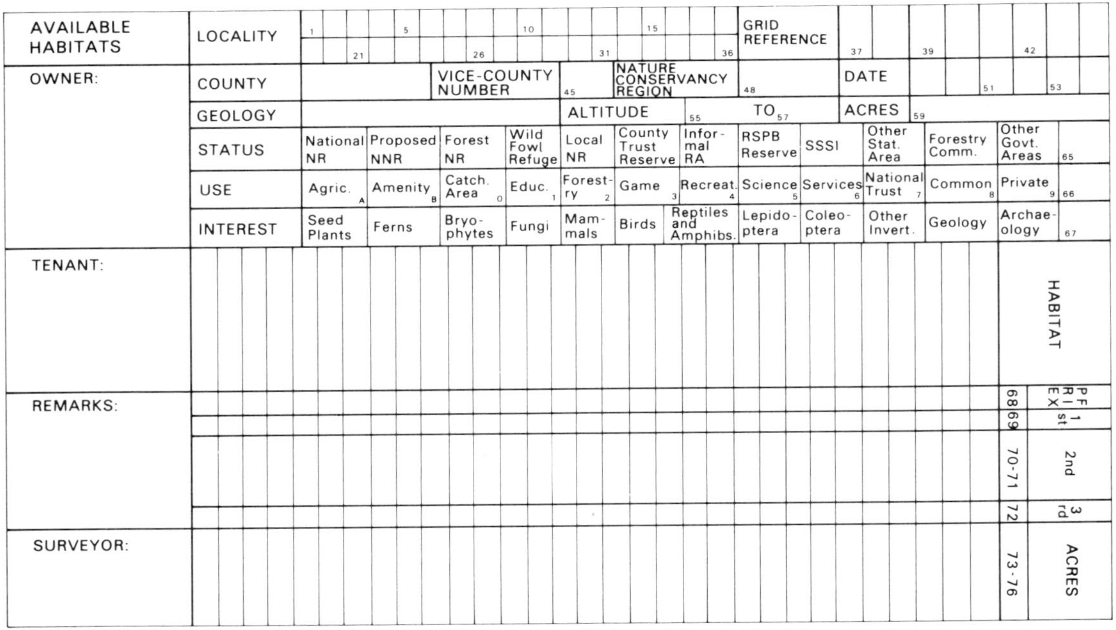

AVAILABLE HABITATS

OWNER:

TENANT:

REMARKS:

SURVEYOR:

LOCALITY 1 5 10 15 21 26 31 36

GRID REFERENCE 37 39 42

COUNTY | VICE-COUNTY NUMBER 45 | NATURE CONSERVANCY REGION 48 | DATE 51 53

GEOLOGY | ALTITUDE 55 TO 57 | ACRES 59

STATUS: National NR | Proposed NNR | Forest NR | Wild Fowl Refuge | Local NR | County Trust Reserve | Informal RA | RSPB Reserve | SSSI | Other Stat. Area | Forestry Comm. | Other Govt. Areas | 65

USE: Agric. A | Amenity B | Catch. Area 0 | Educ. 1 | Forestry 2 | Game 3 | Recreat. 4 | Science 5 | Services 6 | National Trust 7 | Common 8 | Private 9 | 66

INTEREST: Seed Plants | Ferns | Bryophytes | Fungi | Mammals | Birds | Reptiles and Amphibs. | Lepidoptera | Coleoptera | Other Invert. | Geology | Archaeology | 67

HABITAT

PRIEX 68 | 1st 69 | 2nd 70-71 | 3rd 72 | ACRES 73-76

(a)

Figure 20. (a) The habitat card. (The small numbers on the card are to assist the punch card operator and need not concern the recorder.) [*Society for the Promotion of Nature Reserves*[33]]

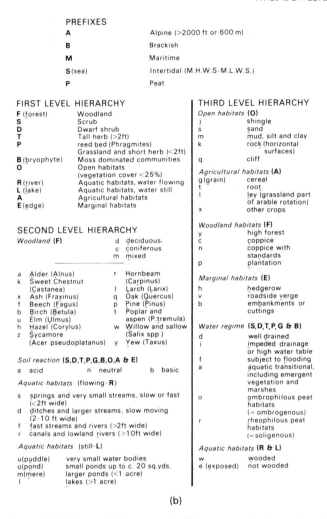

PREFIXES

A	Alpine (>2000 ft or 600 m)
B	Brackish
M	Maritime
S (sea)	Intertidal (M.H.W.S-M.L.W.S.)
P	Peat

FIRST LEVEL HIERARCHY

F (forest)	Woodland
S	Scrub
D	Dwarf shrub
T	Tall herb (>2ft)
P	reed bed (Phragmites)
	Grassland and short herb (<2ft)
B (bryophyte)	Moss dominated communities
O	Open habitats (vegetation cover <25%)
R (river)	Aquatic habitats, water flowing
L (lake)	Aquatic habitats, water still
A	Agricultural habitats
E (edge)	Marginal habitats

SECOND LEVEL HIERARCHY

Woodland (F)

		d	deciduous.
		c	coniferous
		m	mixed

a	Alder (Alnus)	r	Hornbeam (Carpinus)
k	Sweet Chestnut (Castanea)	l	Larch (Larix)
x	Ash (Fraxinus)	q	Oak (Quercus)
f	Beech (Fagus)	p	Pine (Pinus)
b	Birch (Betula)	t	Poplar and aspen (P.tremula)
u	Elm (Ulmus)	w	Willow and sallow (Salix spp.)
h	Hazel (Corylus)	y	Yew (Taxus)
z	Sycamore (Acer pseudoplatanus)		

Soil reaction (S,D,T,P,G,B,O,A & E)

a	acid	n	neutral	b	basic

Aquatic habitats (flowing- **R**)

s	springs and very small streams, slow or fast (<2ft wide)
d	ditches and larger streams, slow moving (2-10 ft wide)
f	fast streams and rivers (>2ft wide)
r	canals and lowland rivers (>10ft wide)

Aquatic habitats (still-**L**)

u (puddle)	very small water bodies
o (pond)	small ponds up to c. 20 sq.yds.
m (mere)	larger ponds (<1 acre)
l	lakes (>1 acre)

THIRD LEVEL HIERARCHY

Open habitats (O)

j	shingle
s	sand
m	mud, silt and clay
k	rock (horizontal surfaces)
q	cliff

Agricultural habitats (A)

g (grain)	cereal
t	root
l	ley (grassland part of arable rotation)
x	other crops

Woodland habitats (F)

y	high forest
c	coppice
n	coppice with standards
p	plantation

Marginal habitats (E)

h	hedgerow
v	roadside verge
b	embankments or cuttings

Water regime (S,D,T,P,G & B)

d	well drained
i	impeded drainage or high water table
f	subject to flooding
a	aquatic transitional, including emergent vegetation and marshes
o	ombrophilous peat habitats (= ombrogenous)
r	rheophilous peat habitats (= soligenous)

Aquatic habitats (R & L)

w	wooded
e (exposed)	not wooded

(b)

Figure 20. (b) Key to habitat symbols. [*Society for the Promotion of Nature Reserves*[32]]

the soil surface, so that a complex community of animal life is able to develop, feeding on dead plants, fungi, and algae growing on the decaying litter, together with other species which are predatory or parasitic on them. In the upper parts of the ungrazed vegetation numerous phytophagous invertebrates are able to exploit the food material in the stems, leaves, flowers, and fruit. M. G. Morris studied the difference between the fauna of grazed and ungrazed chalk grassland with special reference to the leaf hoppers and plant bugs[35]. Twenty-two species of the former and sixteen of the latter occurred more frequently on the ungrazed grassland, while only two species of the former and nine of the latter occurred more abundantly on the grazed area.

Morris also found that the height of the grassland vegetation was closely correlated with the numbers of both individuals and species of certain groups, notably the leafhoppers (Auchenorhyncha), a conspicuous element of the invertebrate fauna[36]. Using a 'vacuum net' apparatus he collected samples of leafhoppers on 2 m², from each of a large number of sites on chalk grassland in southern and eastern England. Figure 21 shows the regression lines he obtained when the number of individuals (a) and species (b) were plotted for each collection against vegetation height. This confirms earlier evidence that, in general, a richer fauna is found in grassland which is not grazed, cut, or trampled.

Spiders are one of the commonest invertebrate groups in grassland litter. On the Hampshire Downs in May, hand-collecting within half square-metre frames produced 6.2 per square metre (mean of 9 samples) on cattle-grazed grassland, and 31.0 per square metre (mean of 11 samples) on ungrazed grassland. Even differences in vegetation height over a small area can produce notable effects. A small patch of *Brachypodium pinnatum* grassland measuring 3 × 2 metres and about 30 cm in height was studied, together with the surrounding rabbit-grazed *Festuca rubra* grassland, which reached about 8 cm in height[37]. Three common Lycosid spiders, *Pardosa nigriceps,* which hunts in the leaf zone and climbs readily, *P. pullata,* a very widespread species which does not climb, and *Alopecosa pulverulenta,* a larger, short-legged species which is partly nocturnal and hunts in the ground vegetation, were collected by means of pitfall traps. Two traps were placed in the *Brachypodium* patch and three in the surrounding vegetation (Figure 22).

In a three-week period the five traps caught 153 specimens of these species distributed as follows:

	Brachypodium 'island' (per cent)	Grazed *Festuca* turf (per cent)
Pardosa nigriceps	92.3	7.7
P. pullata	17.4	82.6
Alopecosa pulverulenta	51.4	48.6

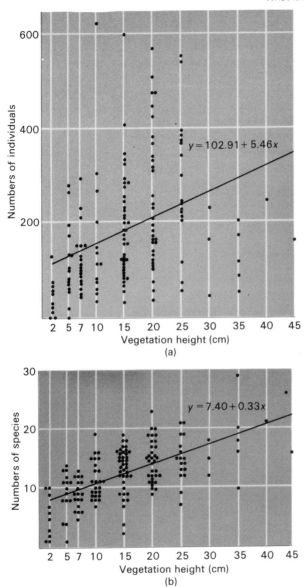

Figure 21. (a) Numbers of individuals of leafhoppers plotted against vegetation height. (b) Numbers of species of leafhoppers plotted against vegetation height. Each dot represents the collection from 2 m² of chalk grassland. [*Morris*[36]]

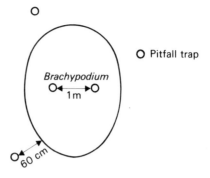

Figure 22. Diagram of *Brachypodium* 'island' and distribution of pitfall traps. [*Duffey*[37]]

Even on this small scale, there is a clear separation between two species (*P. nigriceps* and *P. pullata*) exploiting different parts of the same habitat (in this case limestone grassland). On the other hand *A. pulverulenta* was apparently unaffected by the vertical zonation and structural difference in the vegetation.

Lensink[38] studied the ecology of three species of grasshopper on a sandy heathland area in Holland and found that the conventional methods of plant community description and classification were of little value in defining their respective habitats. He comments that one of the most important and predominant factors in the grasshopper environment is the vegetation, and goes on to say: 'Variations in distribution, however, cannot be explained on the basis of dependence on the vegetation as the food source because in the dune region the insects eat many species of plants and certainly the most frequently occurring species of grasses. What the investigation showed especially clearly was that the structure of the vegetation plays an important part in the distribution observed.' Lensink found it most useful to define the distribution of the grasshoppers in relation to seven vegetation types described in terms of structure (height, density and openness) and five vertical layers.

We can demonstrate this phenomenon more clearly by mapping the distribution of species in relation to the vegetation cover. On a sandy heathland in Denmark a sampling area with sides measuring 2.5 metres was marked out and divided into one hundred 25 × 25 cm squares. A vegetation map was prepared (Figure 23), and showed that most of the

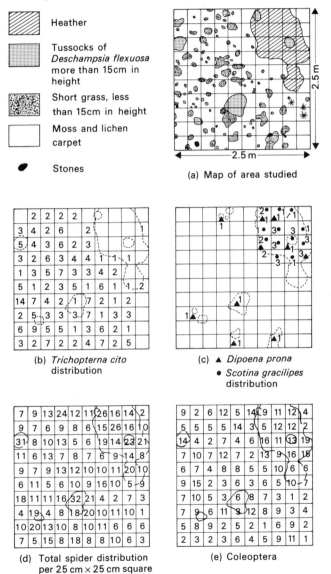

Heather

Tussocks of *Deschampsia flexuosa* more than 15cm in height

Short grass, less than 15cm in height

Moss and lichen carpet

Stones

(a) Map of area studied

(b) *Trichopterna cito* distribution

(c) ▲ *Dipoena prona*
• *Scotina gracilipes* distribution

(d) Total spider distribution per 25 cm × 25 cm square

(e) Coleoptera

Figure 23. Distribution maps of spiders and beetles on a Danish heath. Plot size 2.5 × 2.5 m.

area was covered with a carpet of lichens and mosses, while scattered throughout were small patches of short grass (*Corynephorus canescens*), a few tussocks of a taller grass (*Deschampsia flexuosa*), and, in the top right-hand corner, a patch of heather extending over all, or parts, of eighteen squares (Figure 23 (a)). Each square of vegetation was then carefully cut out, placed in a plastic bag, and taken to the laboratory to be hand-sorted.

The numbers and species of spiders and beetles were then plotted for each of the 100 squares, and some interesting differences emerged (Figure 23 (b)). The small linyphiid spider, *Trichopterna cito,* spins its web between the fronds of lichens, mosses and low grasses, and was obviously able to tolerate the high temperatures and light intensities on the ground. For reasons unknown, the shady, litter-covered ground under heather was avoided. On the extreme right-hand margin of the sampling area this species was recorded in only two out of the ten squares, and on further examination in the field it was found that the squares lay along a little-used track. Trampling had been sufficient to depress but not destroy the lichen and moss growth, but nevertheless had made the micro-habitat unsuitable for *T. cito.* The heather also had its own fauna (Figure 23 (c)). *Dipoena prona* and *Scotina gracilipes* were recorded almost entirely from squares with heather or tall grass tussocks. In Figure 23 (d) and (e) the total spiders and total beetles are recorded for each 25 × 25 cm square, and the highest numbers were found in those with heather or a grass tussock. For instance, square no. 71, which had a tussock of *Deschampsia flexuosa* about 20 cm in diameter, scored a total of 45 spiders and beetles. On the other hand the somewhat larger tussock in squares 25, 26, 35, and 36 scored a high number of spiders (91) but not a particularly high number of beetles (29).

Small habitat differences of this type which can be correlated with changes in the fauna are called micro-habitats, a term which usually corresponds with the meaning of micro-climate, for example the temperature, light, and relative humidity in a small space such as under a stone, in a grass tussock or rabbit hole.

Habitat mosaics and boundaries

Boundaries of macro-habitats ('Edge' in Elton's habitat classification), such as woodland bordering a grassland or heath, are sometimes of great conservation interest but have been the subject of surprisingly little research by biologists. A sharp change from one major formation to another, for example a conifer plantation bordering a cultivated field, would be called an ecotone situation and would have (in this extreme case) no 'edge' definable in terms of wildlife community. A very different 'edge' would be formed by a woodland margin grading into scrub which in turn merges into a field zone and finally grassland. This is called a vegetation ecocline and usually has a flora and fauna with different characteristics from that of the pure stands at either end of the cline. Unfortunately the vegetation ecoline is becoming rare in the modern agricultural landscape where farming methods create sharp boundaries between different habitats.

Certain types of vegetation mosaics which form transition zones may also have distinctive plant and animal associations, as for example an ericaceous heath invading a grassland similar to that studied in Denmark ('field zone' bordering 'open-ground zone' in the Eltonian system). On a coastal system of grass heaths, dunes, and saltmarshes in Germany, Schaeffer[33] showed that the 'edge' habitats or mosaics on the boundaries of these three open-ground types were characterized by the following: (a) eurytopic species reached their optimum; (b) the number of species recorded was higher than in either of the pure stands, and (c) the faunal element of one of the two habitats was usually predominant.

One of the most intensive studies of gradient situations was made on dunes in the Netherlands by van der Maarel[39]. He laid out a 10 x 4 metres transect within a dune slack along which there was a fall in height of 14 cm and a variation in pH from 4.2 to 7.0, following the topographic gradient. In each square metre he counted the number of species of vascular plants, mosses, and lichens. In Figure 24, the contour lines are drawn at 2 cm intervals in height and the squares are shaded according to the number of species present. The highest values are orientated along the middle sections of the elevation and pH gradients.

Van der Maarel commented that (for plants): 'biotic diversity was an expression of environmental diversity, that is, differentiation into micro-habitats or niches', and it was characteristic of a gradient situation that the highest diversity values were found somewhere towards the middle and not at either end. The same situation has been recorded in transects across grassland footpaths where there is a gradient from heavily trampled (centre of path), lightly trampled (margin of path) to undisturbed grassland (beyond path margins). The floristics of each section differ in relation to resistance to trampling and 'competability' of individual species but the highest number of species was recorded in the middle (lightly trampled) zone. This sort of study has never been made

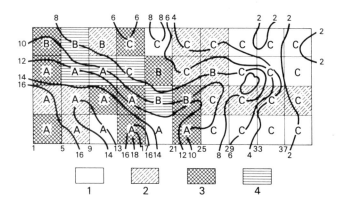

Figure 24. Distribution of species diversity, vegetation types, and height (2 cm contours) in a transect within a dune slack.
Diversity class 1: 17-25 species per square metre; 2: 26-30 sp.; 3: 31-35 sp.; 4: 36-43 sp. A: *Radiola linoides* type; B: *Linum catharticum* type; C: *Parnassia palustris* type. [*van der Maarel*[20]]

for an animal group but the work of Schaeffer and the study of spiders in the Danish heath vegetation mosaic suggest that van der Maarel's conclusions might also apply to the fauna. Further zoological evidence is found in the work of den Boer, also in the Netherlands[40]. He was mainly concerned with factors regulating the populations of species of carabid beetles on a sandy inland heath, but soon found that the species studied did not fit conveniently into definable habitats. His heathland study area included a good deal of vegetational and structural diversity, so that the influence of environmental factors which regulated the animal populations varied from place to place and also from season to season because of climatic differences. In other words habitat heterogeneity on the heathland resulted in some components of the mosaic pattern being more favourable than others for shelter, availability of food, breeding, and so on. This is the same phenomenon as illustrated in Figure 23 (a)-(e) of spiders and beetle distribution on a Danish heath.

Den Boer's study led him to suggest that any particular component in the habitat mosaic might be more favourable biologically (or less favourable) in the following season, for the species of beetles he was studying, because of natural changes in the vegetation and climate. This

constantly varying situation helped to damp down population
fluctuations and maintain a high species diversity and ecological stability.
A botanical situation comparable to this phenomenon had already been
demonstrated by Watt, who developed the now famous 'Pattern and
Process' concept[41]. Watt, in a study of the heathland vegetation in
the East Anglian Breck over many years, showed that the species
composition and structure varied according to age and vigour of the
plants, particularly the dominants. As individual plants died, they
created conditions enabling pioneer species to establish, which in turn
were replaced by others, so that there was a repeated cycle of events
although the heathland area as a whole maintained its characteristic
features. This constantly changing mosaic of plant forms, which may
occur within a few square metres or less, is quite a different process from
natural succession and also from the environmental gradient described
above.

An important part of den Boer's theory, which he called the
'spreading of risk' or the 'risk distribution' theory, was the natural
phenotypic variation found in all populations of animals. Thus some
individuals will be better adapted than others of the same species for
survival in a particular micro-habitat. This characteristic of populations
of species, combined with heterogeneity of habitat, results in differential
survival and helps to spread the risk of possible extinction. This is of
obvious importance in relation to earlier comments on the scientific
assessment of sites for conservation, habitat diversity, size, and
fragmentation of potential reserves.

The diplostenoecious phenomenon

We have suggested in an earlier discussion that one of the characteristics
of rarity is specialization and the more extreme this is, the greater the
threat to survival if the habitat is changed or modified. However, there is
a form of specialization in some species which enables them to become
established in a wider range of habitats than would otherwise appear
possible. I have called this diplostenoecism, which, although rather a long
and awkward word, describes the phenomenon of populations of the
same species occurring in two contrasting types of macro-habitat, for
example marshes and sand dunes[42]. This was first noticed for spiders
over thirty years ago and has since been reported for several species of
insects. The bug *Ischnodemus sabuleti* has attracted attention in North
Germany, where it occurs on dunes and in marshes. After a study of the

biology of this insect, Tischler suggested that although the two biotopes appeared very different, the micro-climate, particularly relative humidity, in a marram tussock on a dune was probably very similar to that in marsh vegetation[43]. The same explanation was offered for those species of spiders which also occurred on dunes and in marshes[44].

However, as more information accumulates on this curious phenomenon, it becomes clear that this suggestion is a quite inadequate explanation. For instance, the linyphiid spider *Hypomma bituberculatum* is a characteristic species of marshy vegetation where the ground is usually waterlogged and a thick, moist litter layer has formed. It is also frequently found on coastal dunes, although only incidentally, in the marram tussocks. In fact it may be more numerous in the *Agropyron* foredunes, where there are no tussocks and no litter over the bare sand, so that the 'comparable micro-climate' explanation would not apply in this case. The lycosid spider *Arctosa perita* excavates a burrow in the mobile sand on yellow dunes, and is also found in the industrial Midlands of England on the coal spoil heaps, where the ground temperatures and relative humidity are probably very different from those on coastal dunes[45].

Erigone arctica is widespread on the open stony tundra above the treeline in Scandinavia. It also occurs on the driftline on the coast, and is commonly found in such situations around Great Britain from Scotland to the Isle of Wight and western Ireland. Although it may be abundant in the drift material on a beach or salt marsh, *E. arctica* has not been recorded inland in Britain except in the stony substrate of sewage filter beds. The stony tundra, a beach drift line, and a sewage filter bed cannot be much more different as habitats, certainly as far as micro-climate is concerned, and yet they must have some features in common. The answer in the case of *A. perita* and *E. arctica* may be due partly to similarity in habitat structure and partly to biotic factors such as competition with related species. *A. perita* requires a soft substrate for burrowing, and on mobile dunes it is usually the only common lycosid. The same type of substrate and absence of potential competitors would be found in coal spoil heaps. The genus *Erigone* includes many closely related species and on German saltmarshes Heydemann has shown, for instance, that when *E. longipalpis* was numerous, *E. arctica* was scarce or absent[46]. Again, the sewage filter bed is a very specialized type of habitat, like the arctic tundra or shoreline drift, and has a very small spider fauna, although the few species present may, in each case, sometimes be very abundant.

Diplostenoecism is a phenomenon which requires much more study, but it appears to include species which perhaps are unusually sensitive to biotic regulators such as competition for food, shelter, and web-building sites, and possibly to parasites and predators. However, providing pressures of this type are sufficiently low, the species may be able to adapt to a wide range of physical environments. This would conform well with the risk distribution theory and again emphasizes the conservation importance of natural diversity in the representation of habitats on nature reserves.

Nevertheless, the conservationist should not overlook the importance of artificial habitats which apparently simulate natural conditions. We have already referred to certain rare Breckland plants which survive only on the disturbed ground of waysides and edges of ploughed fields, although, in general, it is more usual for artificial habitats to be exploited by the commoner plants and animals. The occurrence of *Arctosa perita* on coal spoil heaps in Warwickshire and Leicestershire might have been predicted because of the similarity of substrate texture with that of sand dunes, but the limited distribution of another wolf-spider, *Aulonia albimana,* is difficult to understand. This species is widespread in dry places on the continent of Europe but is only known from one disused gravel pit in this country (Somerset), where it was discovered by W. S. Bristowe in 1936. In spite of repeated searches in similar sites in the region, it has never been found elsewhere. *Lessertia dentichelis,* a distinctive linyphiid spider, is another example of curious habitat selection of man-made situations. In southern Europe, parts of France, the Pyrenees, Italy, and elsewhere, it is only found in natural caves, but further north, although rather rare, it is found in cellars, mines, and drains, and never in natural habitats. In Britain it is very local but has been taken abundantly in some coal-mines and also in sewage filter beds in several places, where it occurs among the pieces of clinker some way beneath the surface, a habitat which it shares with *E. arctica* and a few other species of spiders. The environmental features which all these different habitats probably have in common are darkness, high humidity, stable temperature conditions, and few other species which might be potential competitors.

6

Management as an Ecological Problem

When a nature reserve is established, perhaps the first question we should ask is not what sort of management is necessary, but whether the area needs to be managed at all. We have already seen that natural areas, by definition, do not need intervention by man. Similarly, 'near-natural' formations only need protection from artificial influences likely to cause change, for example, accidental fire, use by too many visitors, pollution carried by drainage water or by air, and introductions of alien plants and animals. In the upland areas of northern England and in Wales and Scotland, these considerations will apply to a wide variety of nature reserves, but in lowland regions, especially the southern half of England, successful wildlife conservation is usually more complicated and concerns different types of problems. A possible exception is mature woodland, which, even though of artificial origin, will change only very slowly providing the timber is not cropped. But an artificial stand is likely to be even-aged so that under-planting will be necessary long before the original trees begin to die if a forest structure is to be maintained.

Lowland grasslands, fens, heaths, some scrublands, and coppice woodlands represented on nature reserves have usually been exploited for many centuries, often passing through cycles of intensive use followed by years of neglect, depending on economic conditions. These deflected climaxes are generally ecologically unstable, so that rapid changes in the fauna and flora may occur following variations in the type and intensity of use. The scientific interest of such a site has been conditioned or even maintained by an ecological history of this sort, so that it is often suggested that the first rule of management should be to continue known traditional practices or, if this is not possible, to simulate them in some way. This is a good general guide and easily understood by reserve staff who are responsible for the practical work. Like most rules, however, it is only partly true. This is because past exploitation was designed to obtain maximum production of a particular crop. For example, a sheep farmer on the downs would wish to stock his grasslands at a higher rate than would be in the best interests of wildlife if the same area was a nature reserve. A reed bed must be cut regularly to maintain its commercial quality and to prevent the accumulation of litter, but 'poor' reed is richer in marshland plants and animals. Maximum production in terms of a crop is therefore incompatible with maximum diversity in terms of wildlife. Even a moorland situation in the Scottish Highlands which is managed for maximum production of red grouse may require drainage, use of fertilizers, and rotational burning of heather, to prevent the plants exceeding about six years of age. This scale of intervention will almost certainly result in changes to the environment of other forms of wildlife, particularly invertebrate animals. It is likely, therefore, that although some species of plants and animals have been preserved by traditional forms of land use, others may have persisted in spite of, rather than as a result of, these practices.

The arguments in favour of traditional practices are often used in the case of woodland nature reserves, where it is thought that past silvicultural management should be continued or simulated. There may be good reasons for this in some modified situations, for example in a wood with an understorey of sweet chestnut (an introduced species), which was originally planted for coppice. Like other vegetation formations, woods have been changed by man over long periods in order to obtain maximum production of useful or saleable material. In a rural economy, where there was a demand for many different products, for example small and large coppice, poles, stakes, posts, firewood, and large timber, the woodland able to meet these needs would also preserve a good deal of biological variety. Today management is based on a much more restricted demand, particularly in the case of hardwoods. Maximum production in terms of commercial exploitation also runs counter to natural processes such as succession. In a mature natural forest more and more energy is channelled, in the course of time, into maintenance or is locked up in dead material. For instance, less than 10 per cent of the annual net production of mature forest is actually consumed by plant-eating animals, so that most of the production is utilized as dead material.

In our discussions on animal habitats, examples were given of specialized species restricted to the dead wood or rotten tree component of a forest, and Elton has described this habitat as one of the two or three greatest resources for the forest animal community. About one-fifth of these species would be lost in a natural woodland if the accumulation of dead material was prevented, and yet this is precisely what tends to happen where there is commercial exploitation for maximum gain.

The same considerations apply to nature reserves popular with the public; maximum recreational use is incompatible with wildlife conservation although some form of controlled access may be acceptable. Management for wildlife is therefore usually a compromise, though often a difficult one. Ecological knowledge of plant and animal communities is still very poor and very few data are available on the influence of factors such as cropping, trampling by the public, pest control, and shooting for sport. Neither do we know much about the indirect effect of building developments, drainage, and industrial activities on adjacent land. All these non-biological factors may influence a nature reserve and yet be outside the control of the reserve manager. To illustrate these points we will examine the history and present-day problems of one of the oldest English nature reserves, Woodwalton Fen in Huntingdonshire (514 acres: 213 ha).

Woodwalton Fen: management for survival

Until the beginning of the seventeenth century, the wide range of peatlands in the Great Fen Basin of East Anglia was still largely unreclaimed. Two hundred years later only a small area remained in the western corner of the Fen Basin centred on a large shallow lake, Whittlesey Mere (Figure 25).

Although Whittlesey Mere still retained a water surface of 1500 acres (640 ha) in the early nineteenth century, it was comparatively shallow and in 1851 the drainage engineer finally achieved its extinction with a new type of steam pump. So disappeared the largest natural lake in lowland England and with it a remarkable wildlife of birds, plants, and insects. More efficient drainage of the surrounding fen now became possible so that cultivation and extensive peat cutting soon followed. It is not known with certainty what use was made at that time of the fenland within the present Nature Reserve, but by the 1870s the parallel east/west drains had been dug to enable peat cutters to boat out their turves to the Great Raveley Drain on the east boundary (Figure 26).

For the remainder of the nineteenth century, peat cutting continued to be the main occupation on the Fen, although a farm incorporated the southern part for grazing, hay-making, and some cultivation in the

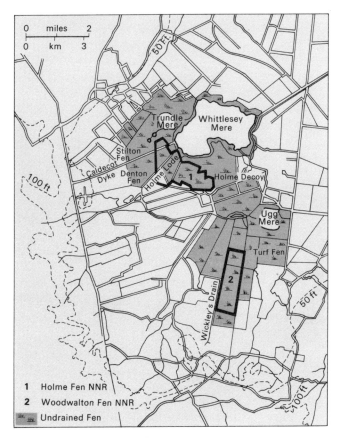

Figure 25. The location of Woodwalton Fen in relation to undrained fenland in 1824. [*Duffey*[47]]

south-eastern compartments. At the close of the peat-cutting phase soon after 1900, the marketable peat had probably been removed and most of the area appears to have been abandoned except as a rough shoot. If we could have visited the scene at the time, we would probably have found a wide open fenland, scarred with the water-filled trenches of abandoned peat cuttings running north-south between the cross drains, beds of reed spreading rapidly over the older cuttings, and a short sedgey vegetation growing on the most recently exposed peat. In 1905 the first eye-witness account described the reserve as consisting mainly of reed with a few

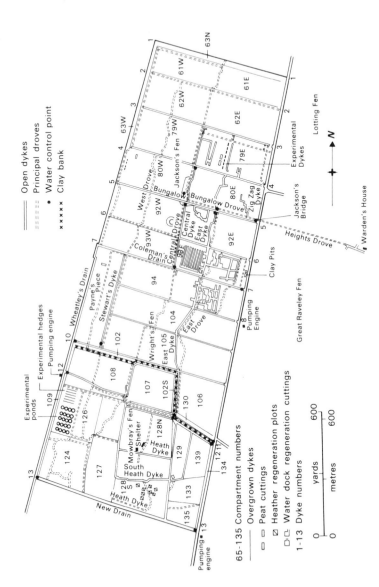

Figure 26. Woodwalton Fen NNR showing the drains, compartments, paths, peat cuttings, and experimental areas. [*Duffey*[47]]

Figure 27. Woodwalton Fen NNR, Hunts. Birch woodland which has developed over *Molinia* fen formerly used for grazing and cutting.

open areas of 'litter' fen, while bush growth was said to be very local. After the nature reserve had been created in 1910, exploitation ceased, apart from reed cutting, which continued on a commercial basis until 1939. By that date bush growth had spread over most of the reserve and this stage in the succession was virtually complete by 1952.

During the same period changes were taking place on land adjacent to the Fen. As peat cutting was abandoned and drainage became more effective, the plough reclaimed the surrounding land, so that by the early 1950s the Reserve was a green rectangular island surrounded by the Black Fen soils. Not only was this much modified fen relict isolated from other semi-natural areas, but it was becoming a plateau raised slightly above the adjacent farmlands. The cultivated peat was shrinking at a faster rate than that on the Fen because of drainage, wind-blow, and oxidation of organic material. Peat shrinkage had in fact been a problem since the drainage of Whittlesey Mere, so that the ground level today, as

Figure 28. Holme Fen post with newly installed post situated on the left. The top (ground level in 1850) of the post is now 12 ft 9 in. (3.92 m) above the present ground surface. Peat shrinkage during the first 25-30 years after the drainage of Whittlesey Mere was rapid but it has been much slower during this century. [*Photo A. V. Fincham*]

demonstrated by the nearby Holme Fen Post (Figure 28), is between 12 and 13 ft (3.6 and 3.9 m) lower than it was in 1851. Some farmland is now well below sea level so that the risk of flooding would be increased if powerful pumps had not been installed to lift water through the various levels in the main drains and finally out to the sea in the Wash.

We can now summarize some of the basic management problems which must be solved if the Fen is to survive.

The water regime

The Reserve lies in a low rainfall area with a mean annual precipitation of about 21.5 in. (546 mm) so that the preservation of marsh conditions prior to 1851 depended on the accumulation of water flowing off the higher lands to the west. The average summer rainfall is 10 in. (242 mm) but because of evaporation losses a further 4.6 in. (115 cm) would be

Figure 29. Woodwalton Fen NNR. New irrigation dyke cut through secondary woodland which has developed over nineteenth century peat cuttings.

needed to maintain a constant water level. This loss is further aggravated by a fall in the mean water level of the Great Raveley Drain from −6 in. (−15 cm) OD in 1900 to −32 in. (−80 cm) OD in 1962[47]. The lower the water level in the Drain, the greater is the loss from the Fen by seepage. Moreover, the Great Raveley Drain water level must continue to fall if the risk of flooding is to be prevented because the land level is also falling with peat wastage.

A plan has now been prepared with the Drainage Authority whereby during periods of heavy rain the Fen will serve as a wash, absorbing flood water which would otherwise spread over surrounding agricultural land. In return the Drainage Authority will clay-core the banks of the reserve to prevent loss by seepage. This plan includes provision for drainage water to be channelled through the Fen so that it can be used to maintain an adequate water table during dry seasons. It will be some years before the whole scheme is complete but it seems to be the only hope for long-term survival of the Fen wildlife communities. Nevertheless some risk is also involved. Although some degree of winter flooding was probably an annual event in pre-drainage times, it is likely that flood levels in the future will rise much more quickly as excess drainage water is directed to the Fen, far greater depths will accumulate and flooding over the Reserve is likely to be total rather than patchy. The effect that this will have on the fauna and flora is unknown, but if the proposed scheme is rejected the only alternative is for the Fen gradually to dry out and a woodland to develop.

The fauna and flora

The first object of management in the Nature Conservancy's Management Plan for Woodwalton Fen is: 'to create and maintain an adequate range of habitat types necessary for the conservation of the characteristic plant and animal associations and rare species of special scientific interest on the Fen'. The water regime necessary for this seems to be assured, but what is meant by the 'characteristic' plants and animals? Peat cutting during the second half of the nineteenth century stripped off nearly all the surface acid peat, together with its flora of mosses, sedges, and dwarf shrubs[48]. Only a few species—heather, cross-leaved heath, sawsedge, sweet gale, and dwarf sallow, which were able to tolerate the drier conditions—have survived to the present day and are now confined almost entirely to one compartment. Elsewhere a secondary flora of common species has spread over the exposed peat so that it is difficult to define what is meant by 'characteristic' species. The Fen flora is notable for its almost complete absence of the rare plants typical of other East Anglian fenlands, with the exception of *Ranunculus lingua.* The rare plants which do occur on the Reserve are therefore not characteristic fen species, although the fen violet *Viola stagnina* (see Figure 18) grew on Wicken Fen fifty years ago and on Lakenheath Poors Fen in West Suffolk until the area was reclaimed in the 1950s. The fen violet and the other rarities, *V. canina* ssp. *montana, Luzula pallescens,* and *Dianthus armeria,* are all plants which normally grow in relatively open situations, soon disappearing if the taller common plants are not controlled. Some progress is being made in achieving the necessary control by clearing bush growth, making shallow peat cuttings, re-excavating dykes, mowing, and cattle grazing—all management techniques which attempt to recreate former habitat conditions.

The fauna of Woodwalton Fen has also been well studied and data are available on 21 invertebrate and 5 vertebrate orders. The best known are the birds, butterflies and moths, beetles, sawflies, dragonflies, and spiders.

Figure 30. Recording germination of seedling heather plants on pathway through Woodwalton Fen.

The 665 species of moths and butterflies and 750 species of beetles include several rarities, but they are species which are also known from other East Anglian fens. There is no evidence of faunal relics from these groups comparable with the plants which would provide a link with the pre-drainage bog conditions. The exception is the famous large copper butterfly, described later (page 106). The spider fauna also has a number of rarities including the large wolf spider, *Lycosa paludicola,* which is not known from any other site in East Anglia. In Somerset and many places on the continent, however, it is associated with acid peat areas, so that at Woodwalton Fen it may be a genuine relict of the primeval fauna.

Defining objectives

The conservation of Woodwalton Fen seen in the context of the discussions in earlier chapters is a particularly difficult scientific as well as technical problem, because subjective criteria influence the definition of long-term objectives. This is likely to be true for many semi-natural areas, but at Woodwalton Fen we have the unusual situation of having lost not only most of the original vegetation, but also the substrate on which it grew, so that the gradual restoration of the former condition is not possible. In theory, therefore, there are several choices available, each of which could be supported by good scientific arguments. We could allow normal succession to take place and record the change in the fauna and flora as woodland developed. If, on the other hand, we feel it would be of greater value for wildlife conservation to maintain fen conditions, assuming that the technical problem of conserving a high water table can be solved, we must be able to answer the question: What type of fen ecosystem would be appropriate? We are not able to recreate the primeval conditions for reasons already stated. If peat cutting were re-introduced on the grounds that it was a traditional land-use practice, the resources would soon be exhausted because the remaining deposit of peat is now thin. The reserve could be cleared of trees and bushes and an open herbaceous vegetation maintained similar to that which seems to have existed at the end of the nineteenth century. However, the expense would be enormous, both for the initial clearance and for subsequent maintenance to prevent the re-invasion of woody species. In addition this proposal would also reduce the potential biological diversity.

Our remaining alternative is to maintain a balance between existing habitats, extending some (open water, marsh, and herbaceous fen), and reducing others (mainly bush growth of non-fen species and sallow carr). Within this general pattern, special regimes to maintain habitat conditions for the surviving species of special ecological interest would be imposed, together with research to improve our ability to do this. Exponents of 'naturalness' would criticize this management objective as creating an entirely artificial situation almost comparable with gardening. My answer would be that it is the most interesting and economical way of making the best use of what has survived on Woodwalton Fen and that the same criteria must in fact be applied to all reserves which fall within our definition of 'semi-natural'.

Grasslands and scrub: management for diversity

Grasslands are one of the most widespread and important types of vegetation cover in Britain, accounting for about 62 per cent (45.5 million acres: 19 million ha) of all land in agricultural use. Nearly two-thirds of this total consists of rough grazings, mainly in upland regions, and the remainder is classified as permanent grassland, an agricultural term which includes swards more than seven years old. However, permanent pasture on lowland grassland nature reserves is generally very much older than this and represents a semi-natural rather than an artificial formation, as, for example, the grasslands on chalk

Figure 31. Cleeve Hill, Gloucestershire. Limestone grassland.

downs. Indeed, archaeologists have produced some evidence that
grasslands on the best-preserved Celtic field systems of the chalk may
not have been ploughed for a thousand years or more.

Calcicolous grasslands are best represented, and richest in plant species,
on the chalk soils of southern England, but other important and
distinctive types occur on the oolitic (Jurassic) limestone which lies on
the northern boundary of the chalk, carboniferous limestone mainly in
the north and west, magnesian limestone forming a narrow strip from
Nottingham to Durham, and the very limited outcrops of Devonian
limestone on parts of the south coast (Figure 32). Many basic ideas
about plant communities on the chalk and limestone were developed in

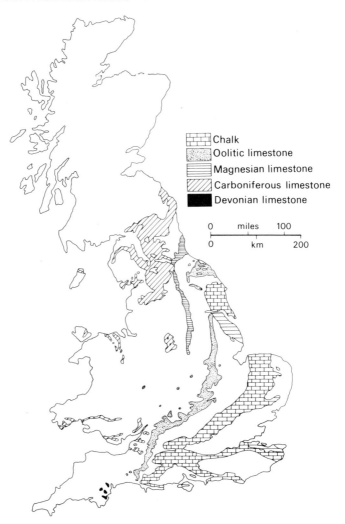

Figure 32. The distribution of major calcareous rock formations in England and Wales.

the early years of this century, when grasslands were more widespread and not fully exploited or properly managed because of the agricultural depression. It seems probable that what we now consider to be 'good' calcicolous grassland is derived from the conditions of that time and consequently represents a particular phase in ecological history.

Figure 33. Wye and Crundale Downs NNR, Kent. Situated on the escarpment of the North Downs between Ashford and Canterbury, this fine nature reserve includes chalk grassland, scrub and mature woodland. The view in this picture shows the steep-sided valley known as the Devil's Kneading Trough. [*Photo P. Wakeley*]

Chalk grassland is the most extensive and the best studied of these types, but a rapid decline in total area has taken place, particularly since the mid-1940s, when agricultural subsidies and guaranteed prices made it profitable to reclaim the Downs for arable farming. In 1966 it was estimated that of $3\frac{1}{4}$ million acres (1.3 million ha) of land on chalk soils, only 107 000 acres (44 583 ha) still had unenclosed and untilled grassland, and 80 per cent of this occurred in Wiltshire, Dorset, and Hampshire. Wiltshire has, in fact, much more surviving chalk grassland than any other county, mainly because the Ministry of Defence controls large areas of Salisbury Plain. Its 73 000 acres (30 450 ha) of permanent chalk grassland are distributed between 529 sites, of which 500 average about 50 acres (20 ha) in area. Nearly all the flat or gently sloping sites have been cultivated, so that of the survivors there is a preponderance of steep scarp slopes where the plough cannot operate. The few sites on more level ground may be of outstanding interest for other reasons as well as their scientific value. The Fyfield Down NNR (612 acres: 255 ha) is famous for its Sarcen stones (sandstone blocks) which lie scattered over the chalk, creating local pockets of acid soil. It is also one of the richest archaeological sites on the chalk with a dozen or more remains of prehistoric and Romano-British settlements.

As suggested elsewhere, archaeological studies on long-established grasslands may be of particular value to the ecologist in helping to date certain types of plant communities. If ploughing or other disturbance is very ancient, for example Celtic fields, or perhaps no later than medieval, as seems to be the case of Upwood Meadows (page 15), so that reinvasion by the original flora has had plenty of time to take place, the community may regain most of its former species. This would depend, of course, on a form of management which retains a grass sward. However, cultivation usually means complete destruction, especially with modern techniques such as deep ploughing followed by treatment with chemical fertilizers and selective herbicides. Recently reverted grasslands on abandoned arable land or sown leys are usually recognizable because they contain only common plants, the dominants of which are species with a high competitive ability, often demonstrated by a fast growth rate and by reaching a height which overshadows associated species. On the other hand, long-established grassland is more likely to have rare and local species as well as being characterized by greater floristic richness. However, the development of species richness in relation to age of sward depends on many factors and few studies have been made.

Neutral grassland

Neutral grassland is a term first used by Tansley to include semi-natural grasslands occurring on soil neither markedly alkaline nor very acid, and mostly developed on clays and loams. Until recently these grasslands had been very much neglected by botanists and conservationists, and relatively few survive today. They are particularly vulnerable to agricultural improvement, drainage, and cultivation, so that survival has been due mainly to chance or because the ownership is held by an older-generation farmer who does not use modern methods. This problem is not confined to Britain. A recent survey in Sweden[49] has

shown that large areas of marshy meadows have been abandoned for
stock rearing and the land neglected or used for other purposes such as
dumping rubbish, building, golf courses, and tree planting. The total area
of old pasture and meadow fell from 2.47 million acres (1.03 million ha)
in 1932 to 576 000 acres (240 000 ha) in 1969, and is now causing great
concern to both conservationist and sportsman because of the loss of
breeding and feeding habitats for marshland birds.

Some fourteen types of neutral grassland have been described in
Britain, ranging from herbaceous marshes on silts and peats to grasslands
on alluvial soils, clays and sands. It is sometimes difficult to separate
them from other grasslands because they may grade into calcareous
swards or into scrub, or in another direction into richer types of mires.
Only the more important types can be described here.

The East Anglian washes

These specialized meadow systems are associated with long-established
flood relief schemes in the Fenland Basin. Few remain today but the
largest and most important are the Ouse Washes, extending for over 5300
acres (2208 ha) between two artificial drainage channels called the New
and Old Bedford Rivers. In most years the land is flooded from
November to March and, because this has been more or less an annual
event since about the seventeenth century, a distinctive flora has
developed. Of particular interest are the sixteen species and hybrids of
Potamogeton growing in the ditches and drains. However, by far the
greatest interest of these Washlands are the remarkable numbers of wild
duck, geese, and swans which can be seen in winter and on migration. Of
equal interest is the summer breeding bird population, including scarce
species such as garganey, gadwall and pintail. The Washes are also the
most important breeding area of the black-tailed godwit and the only
British site where the ruff and black tern have bred in recent years.

Alluvial meadows

In some of the flood plains of river valleys in lowland Britain, a very
small number of meadows still survive which have a strikingly rich and
attractive flora. One of the best examples is at Cricklade in Wiltshire,
where the snakeshead carpets many acres of meadow with flowers of
different shades. By the Thames near Oxford are the Yarnton and Pixey
Meads, and the famous Port Meadow, both sites of great interest because

the same management has been continued for centuries. The former are cut out for hay and the latter are grazed.

Old ridge and furrow pasture

These grasslands occur on clays and lighter soils, most of which have again been ploughed or greatly altered by agricultural 'improvement' in recent years. One of the best examples, at Upwood in Huntingdonshire, has been referred to on page 15. There, 112 species of vascular plants have been recorded on 14 acres (5.8 ha), while in Suffolk there survives a small but splendidly colourful *Colchicum* (autumn crocus) meadow, a type which has now become very rare.

Northern hay and grazing meadows

There are several types of old enclosed pasture in northern England, Wales, and Scotland, including many characteristic of the drift soils derived from carboniferous limestone in the upland valleys and lower hill slopes in Westmorland, Yorkshire, and Upper Teesdale. Some fine examples of a tall herb community also survive on the ungrazed river banks of the Tees, Tyne, Tay, Irthing, and Lochay.

   In spite of a great increase in knowledge of neutral grasslands in recent years, they are probably the most threatened of British habitats and still poorly known compared with other types of grasslands. There is at present only one neutral grassland National Nature Reserve, and some other areas are protected by voluntary conservation bodies.

Managing grasslands

The terms 'pasture' and 'meadow' are often used as if their meanings were synonymous and botanical texts do not usually attempt to define them. However, I think it is useful to follow Ellenberg and Mueller-Dombois[50], who adopted what were probably the original meanings, that is, 'pasture' describes grasslands below the tree line which were used primarily for grazing, and 'meadow' refers to those whose main purpose was the production of hay. These two uses are, of course, often combined. There may be spring grazing followed by a summer hay crop, or—more commonly—a hay crop followed by grazing of the aftermath. Both these combinations have important influences on the vegetation and floristics. Nevertheless, in most cases the *main* function of a particular grassland is likely to be one or other use, and the terms 'meadow' and 'pasture' should be read in this sense.

Calcicolous grasslands have been conditioned very largely by many centuries of sheep grazing, and also rabbit grazing, although this animal did not become an important biotic factor until the sixteenth century and later[51]. Both animals crop the grass very closely, so that the chalk downs and the Breckland grass heaths before myxomatosis were characterized by short open swards, often with a good deal of bare ground if grazing was intense. Trampling by sheep, cattle, and horses, and scratching and burrowing by rabbits, are biotic factors which cannot be separated from grazing when assessing the influence of these animals on the vegetation. These herbivores not only crop down the vegetation and select out the more palatable species, but, by creating bare or disturbed ground, provide a habitat for low-growing or prostrate plants and a seed bed for many annuals.

The highest numbers of species of plants per unit area on calcicolous grasslands are recorded from short grazed swards (Figure 34) so that continuation of traditional use is important for conservation. In the absence of grazing, grasses increase in leaf area and height so that many of the low-growing perennials and annuals may be suppressed or even eliminated after a few years. In other cases, for example the pasque flower, the plants may continue to spread by vegetative reproduction, but the proportion able to flower falls off rapidly (Table 4).

Table 4. Behaviour of the pasque flower *Pulsatilla vulgaris* within an enclosure of 42 x 12 m from 1964-70, in relation to height of vegetation. [Wells[34]]

	1964	1965	1966	1967	1968	1969	1970
Total no. of plants	138	469	612	849	760	654	505
% flowering	65.0	62.0	9.3	10.8	6.8	6.0	5.5
Height of grasses (cm)	6.9	10.1	15.2	20.3	17.8	22.0	25.0

T. C. E. Wells[52] has pointed out that over 90 per cent of chalk grassland plants are perennials, suggesting that this characteristic of the vegetation community has evolved in relation to the biotic factor of grazing. Those plants which are best adapted to tolerate repeated defoliation, or with behavioural or structural devices for avoiding it, have been most successful in establishing themselves as permanent members of the community. Vegetative means of reproduction are widely used by

Figure 34. Barnsey Warren, Gloucestershire. Plant recording on limestone grassland.

grassland plants when flower and seed production are prevented by grazing. Even when quantities of viable seed are produced, as in the case of the pasque flower, seedlings are rarely found, possibly because germination conditions are often unfavourable. Longevity is another important characteristic of grassland plants. Wells[53] has shown that individual plants of the autumn lady's tresses (*Spiranthes spiralis*) on the Knocking Hoe NNR may be at least 22 years old, and that the population he studied, which increased vegetatively at about 5 per cent per annum, could have been in existence for over 100 years. Harper and White[54], after studying extensive data from meadow grassland, concluded that long life and vegetative reproduction are characteristics of meadow perennials and that establishment by seed is rare.

Grasses are also the main contributors to the formation of the litter layer in ungrazed grassland, which suppresses the growth of dwarf plants and prevents germination. The re-introduction of grazing soon breaks up and disperses the litter and reduces vegetation height. At Aston Rowant NNR, where *Arrhenatherum elatius* and *Brachypodium sylvaticum* were dominants, Wells showed that a stocking density of 1.2 sheep per ha reduced the sward height from 47 cm to 7 cm after 4 years[55].

Cutting is an entirely different process from grazing: there is no trampling effect, no return of nutrients in the form of dung and urine, and it is entirely non-selective. However, by opening up the sward and reducing the competitive ability of dominant grasses, it helps to maintain floristic richness. Cutting in spring, during the period of maximum growth, was found to be more effective in suppressing the vigorous grass *Bromus erectus* than cutting at any other time of the year, but the best control was obtained by three cuts in April, June, and July.

On alluvial grasslands spring grazing would be very destructive to the snakeshead, the plant being sensitive to trampling, while in *Colchicum* meadows it is the practice to defer grazing until after the hay crop has been harvested to allow the poisonous leaves of this plant to die down.

Agronomists have experimented for many years on the floristic changes in grasslands which follow the application of fertilizers, particularly nitrogen, phosphorus, potassium, and calcium. The most famous example is the Park Grass Experiment at Rothamsted, which began in 1856. These plots were first managed by taking a hay crop followed by sheep grazing, but after 1873 grazing was discontinued and a second hay crop subsituted. Each treatment is now represented by a unique species composition contrasting sharply with each other and the control plot. The very extensive work which has been done since on the effects of mineral nutrition was designed to find ways of increasing the productivity and value of the sward for stock rearing. This is a very different objective from that of the conservationist, who wishes to preserve species and communities which, in many cases, are associated with nutrient-*poor* substrates. It is claimed, for example, that low fertility of chalk soils, especially with respect to nitrogen, is directly related to high floristic diversity in the grass sward. Improvements in fertility levels are often brought about by successional changes which lead to bush colonization, and this may lead to a loss in richness of plant species[56]. Nevertheless, because species composition of grasslands can be altered or regulated by the use of chemicals or by a combination of chemicals and a particular grazing regime, this form of management may become a valuable tool for conservation. Its use today is limited by the inadequate knowledge of the precise effects on semi-natural plant communities. The same is true for selective herbicides which are also powerful agents for influencing the status of species in grasslands.

Another aspect of this problem, which concerns the conservationist and is currently being studied by D. A. Wells at the Monks Wood Experimental Station, is the degree of tolerance shown by certain rare or important plants to fertilizer treatments. This is now a real problem in the case of meadow grasslands, most of which are unfortunately not controlled by any conservation body. These areas are nearly always of considerable agricultural value, and by applying the appropriate chemicals it is comparatively easy to increase the proportion and the growth of 'useful' grasses and to reduce or eliminate other species. It is possible, however, that a compromise may be achieved between the agronomist and the conservationist if it can be demonstrated that, up to a certain level of fertilizer application, production can be increased but the status of particular plants, for example the snakeshead, is not endangered.

Grassland management and the fauna

Semi-natural grasslands have been studied fairly intensively by the botanist but zoological data are much more scattered and fragmentary. Grassland management for animals is therefore less well understood, although the agricultural zoologist has made comprehensive studies on soil faunas, mainly in connection with pest control. An ornithological example for the Norfolk Breckland has already been mentioned (pages 20-21), an enclosed rabbit population recreating favourable nesting conditions for stone curlews and wheatears. In the Ouse Washes of the Fenland Basin, grazing and trampling by cattle helps to maintain a mosaic of short and long vegetation and muddy places which provide feeding and breeding sites for lapwings, redshanks, and black-tailed godwits. No experimental work has been done on this interesting problem, however.

Rather more is known about the effects of different management treatments on the invertebrate fauna. The work of M. G. Morris[36, 57] on the responses of certain insect groups of calcicolous grasslands to grazing and cutting has been particularly valuable, but only a brief summary is possible here. The fauna can be grouped into four main components: (a) phytophagous species feeding on a particular plant or group of plants; (b) predators usually ranging fairly widely over the different micro-

habitats in search of prey; (c) saprophagous species feeding on
breakdown products of dead organic material; and (d) species parasitic
on other animals, sometimes showing high specificity to a particular
host.

All these groups are influenced at some stage in their life cycle by the
growth form of the vegetation, which determines the local microclimate
and other environmental factors. In terms of vertical zones, a grass sward
consists of the root zone below the soil surface, a humus layer, the litter
layer and stem bases of growing plants, the leaf zone, and the upper stem
zone with flowers and seeds. When grazing or cutting takes place, the
upper layers of this series are immediately reduced, especially the flowers
and the seed. Table 5 shows the results obtained by Morris, who
compared the total numbers of selected invertebrate groups extracted
from turf samples taken from grazed and ungrazed chalk grassland.

Table 5. Total number of representatives of selected invertebrate groups extracted
from turf samples taken on 14 occasions, 2 November, 1966, to 9 October, 1967.
(8 m² removed from both grazed and ungrazed chalk grassland.) [Morris[57]]

	Grazed	Ungrazed
Gastropoda	83	171
Isopoda	22	594
Chilopoda-Lithobiomorpha	601	2664
Diplopoda-Polydesmidae	178	910
Araneae	177	2023
Lepidoptera larvae	82	76
Coleoptera adults	654	1949
Coleoptera larvae	612	566

The magnitude of these differences will vary according to type of
grassland; on some poor soils, ungrazed or uncut grassland may never
grow tall and the litter layer is relatively insignificant. In some cases,
fairly heavy grazing may gradually change the composition of the sward
so that a taller, denser growth develops rather than the reverse process.
For example, on drift soils near Malham Tarn, Yorkshire, the tough
unpalatable grass *Nardus stricta* invaded an *Agrostis/Festuca* pasture
which had been depressed by heavy sheep grazing. An examination of
the spider fauna in this mosaic clearly showed that there was a richer
fauna with a higher number of individuals in the *Nardus* tussocks
(Figure 35)[58] than in the areas between. Luff[59] has also shown that the
micro-climate of *Dactylis glomerata* tussocks differed from that in the
nearby short grass and provided a habitat for certain Coleoptera.

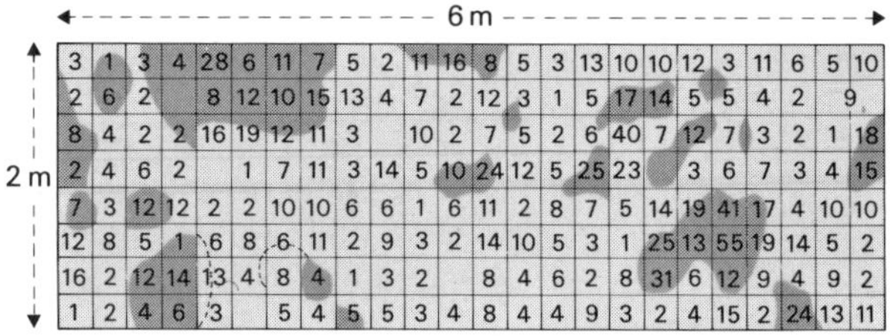

← - - - - - - - - - - - - - - - 6 m - - - - - - - - - - - - - - - →

3	1	3	4	28	6	11	7	5	2	11	16	8	5	3	13	10	10	12	3	11	6	5	10
2	6	2		8	12	10	15	13	4	7	2	12	3	1	5	17	14	5	5	4	2	9	
8	4	2	2	16	19	12	11	3		10	2	7	5	2	6	40	7	12	7	3	2	1	18
2	4	6	2		1	7	11	3	14	5	10	24	12	5	25	23		3	6	7	3	4	15
7	3	12	12	2	2	10	10	6	6	1	6	11	2	8	7	5	14	19	41	17	4	10	10
12	8	5	1	6	8	6	11	2	9	3	2	14	10	5	3	1	25	13	55	19	14	5	2
16	2	12	14	13	4	8	4	1	3	2		8	4	6	2	8	31	6	12	9	4	9	2
1	2	4	6	3		5	4	5	5	3	4	8	4	4	9	3	2	4	15	2	24	13	11

↕ 2 m

Figure 35. Total spiders taken in each $\frac{1}{16}$ m² from 6 x 2 m of grassland at Malham. Grass tussocks, mainly *Nardus*, over 5 cm indicated by shaded areas. [*Duffey*[58]]

Reference should also be made to pages 66-67 [Figure 21(a) and (b)] in which Morris[36] has demonstrated a general relationship between vegetation height and numbers of individuals and species of leafhoppers.

Nevertheless, although a short cropped vegetation has a poorer fauna, certain species of animals are confined to situations with sparse open vegetation and patches of bare ground. Such species tend to disappear when the vegetation becomes thicker and taller. This occurred in the Breckland grass heaths after myxomatosis. Open ground species of spiders, notably *Attulus saltator* and *Arctosa perita*, became very scarce as the bare sandy areas were vegetated. On ground of this type there is also a high insolation effect and it has been suggested that thermophilous Heteroptera at the edge of their range in Britain are able to survive on chalk and sandy soils where these microclimatic conditions are found.

The seasonal aspects of grazing and its influence on the invertebrate fauna are not yet well understood. Autumn and winter grazing on nature reserves is to be preferred because a grassland which is rested or only very lightly grazed during the summer preserves the many insects which feed on its flowers and seeds. Meadow faunas have been poorly studied in comparison with other grasslands but available evidence suggests that the number of animals and the species diversity may be low. If this proves to be the case, a possible reason may be the drastic change to the environment which takes place each year when the hay is cut, followed by grazing. The removal of most of the vegetation, exposing the ground surface to sun and wind, may prevent more specialized and sensitive species from establishing themselves.

Grazing or cutting for hay also prevents the build-up of litter and the rich fauna associated with it (page 99). When litter is trampled, its structure is broken down and the invertebrate community is largely destroyed. Even when trampling is comparatively light, marked changes may take place in the numbers and representation of different animal groups. For example, in Table 6 differences between the faunas of trampled and untrampled litter are shown for an experimental grass ley. Trampling in this case consisted of one tread by the foot of a medium-sized man, twice per day for five consecutive days, each month over a year. The annual total of 120 treads made very little difference to the vegetation but reduced the population of several animal groups.

Table 6. The influence of treading on some invertebrate groups in grassland litter.

	Control (means of 23 samples)	10 'treads' during each of 12 months (means of 25 samples)
Annelida	20.2	18.1
Coleoptera	80.1	12.8
Araneae	11.0	1.8
Isopoda	16.5	0.3
Molluscs	13.5	5.2
Diptera larvae	25.0	46.2

The problem of meeting the management objectives of the grassland botanist and the grassland zoologist may sometimes appear complicated or even contradictory. On some grasslands of low productivity, light grazing may produce a mosaic of short and long vegetation and so would maintain suitable conditions for the fauna as well as the flora. However, where grazing results in a uniformly open, low sward, many animal species will be scarce or disappear. Perhaps the best arrangement is a form of rotational grazing or cutting as suggested by Dr Morris. Short and long rotations are proposed within the same area, while adjacent areas may be continuously grazed or regularly cut. Ungrazed grassland is, of course, a temporary condition because normal succession leads to invasion by scrub. The long rotation would therefore be based on the length of time which elapses before growth appears.

The scrub habitat

For many years ecologists and conservationists have neglected scrublands, and this habitat has only been preserved incidentally on

Figure 36. Aston Rowant NNR, Oxfordshire. This attractive reserve in the Chilterns is well known for its chalk grassland and species-rich scrub which includes juniper (in the picture), wayfaring tree, hawthorn, privet, buckthorn, dogwood, yew, and whitebeam. Recently the reserve has been split into two parts by the extension of the M40 motorway which cuts through the chalk ridge. [*Photo P. Wakeley*]

reserves established for other reasons. It is, perhaps, unfortunate that in too many instances scrub has appeared on sites where it was not wanted, particularly grassy and heathy places. Consequently accounts dealing with scrub management have usually only described methods of getting rid of it.

Scrub varies in species composition according to soil, aspect, altitude and past management. On calcareous soils in southern Britain, rich mixtures may develop of hawthorn, dogwood, rose, brambles, wayfaring tree, privet, hazel, blackthorn, yew, and juniper. On neutral soils, hawthorn, blackthorn, birch, and elder may be common, while on more acid soils, gorse, broom, birch, and pine often predominate. Most scrub mixtures occur as marginal formations to other habitats, for example on scarp slopes too steep to graze or cut. Elsewhere scrub develops temporarily on abandoned grassland and heath or after a woodland has been clear-felled. Some species may form almost pure stands, notably juniper, yew, box, and sea buckthorn among the less common, and hawthorn, blackthorn and gorse among those more widespread. A similar type of great interest is the hazel scrub on the limestone Karst of western

Ireland. Scrub plants are often of great importance for agricultural or economic reasons, for example, hedgerows, shelter belts, windbreaks, and bush growth preserved for game management or planted for landscaping.

The more common scrub species have a rich entomological fauna associated with the wood, leaves, flowers, and fruit. Brightly coloured, fleshy fruits are characteristic of many, and are much sought after by resident and migrant thrushes and the waxwing. The large number of seeds eaten by these birds is believed to be an important factor in aiding the dispersal of scrub species to new sites. Breeding birds may also be abundant in scrub, particularly if the growth is dense and consists of spiny species such as gorse. A survey of 200 acres (83 ha) of hawthorn scrub on Irvinghoe Hill in Buckinghamshire, by K. Williamson, recorded 540 pairs of breeding birds, represented by 36 species[60].

Data on the invertebrates associated with scrub plants are scattered, but it is known that the fauna of some is much richer than others. T. R. E. Southwood[61] has suggested that the longer a woody species has been a native of Britain, the more likely it is to have a rich fauna. Not all native species follow this rule, for example juniper, yew, and box which have few specialized species of insects and arachnids which are more or less confined to them. A detailed study has been made of the fauna of juniper by L. K. Ward[62], who found that species richness was closely related to the number and the age of bushes in each colony. For example, juniper does not appear to fruit until it is ten to fifteen years old, so that fruit- and seed-eating insects will be late immigrants during the development of the colony.

Where scrub is already well established, and the object of management is to maintain this habitat, Dr Ward has suggested that rotational cutting is the best method. This has the advantage of preserving the seral stage of scrub succession and the different floras and faunas associated with them. Cutting should take place when some grass cover is still locally present, although in some cases it may be necessary to preserve a scrub thicket for nesting birds. Fairly large blocks of at least an acre should be treated at any one time. After clearance, the succeeding grass sward phase should be maintained by grazing or mowing for a few years to enable the less common scrub species to reach the site. In general, however, the recolonizing species will be derived from the nearest parent seed source. The same will apply to areas of grass heath, and old arable land where new scrub is allowed to develop, although the soil type and the past use of the site also influence the species composition.

Management for selected species.

The published reasons for nature reserve establishment frequently include reference to species of animals and plants which are rare or of special ecological interest. In the early days of conservation such criteria would often provide the sole basis for protecting an area. Nevertheless, autecological studies designed to find out how to maintain, increase, or re-establish these species are very few. Perhaps more examples are known among birds than other groups, and some of the best-known include the management of Havergate Island for the avocet, and Minsmere for the marsh harrier and avocet. Apart from reducing disturbance and interference, which are very important factors as far as successful breeding in birds is concerned (for instance the red kite in Wales), the achievements have been due to management technology based on good ecological guesses rather than on detailed biological or experimental studies. However, there is now such a large volume of scientific literature on British breeding birds, which only number just over 200 species, that this *ad hoc* approach to management can perhaps be justified when this great accumulation of knowledge is combined with long practical experience. It is less straightforward for the 2000 British vascular plants—and for the 25 000 invertebrate species, the reliability of ecological guesswork is even more fragile.

Some plants of the open ground zone

One of the earliest and smallest nature reserves was established in Gloucestershire for the adder's tongue spearwort, *Ranunculus ophioglossifolius,* which is known from only one other British locality[63] It grows on the bare mud around a small pond and soon disappears if smothered by other vegetation. By cutting the tall plants and clearing away the accumulated litter and debris to expose the bare ground, the Gloucestershire Trust for Nature Conservation in 1962/63 created favourable conditions for seed germination in an area where the plant had not been seen since 1938. They also showed that the seedlings, which germinate in the autumn, are particularly susceptible to frosts, but that if the pond water level is sufficiently high to submerge them, then mortality is greatly reduced.

Another plant associated with disturbed ground in moist places is the rare fen violet *Viola stagnina* (see Figure 18) at Woodwalton Fen. It was formerly widespread in the boggy ground around Whittlesey Mere in the early nineteenth century, and was known to grow on recently abandoned peat cuttings at Woodwalton. As the reserve became covered with tall .ierbs and bushes, the fen violet became very scarce and only survived in the short vegetation of mown pathways and in grassy areas grazed by rabbits. In 1954 a number of shallow peat cuttings were made and work was started on the re-excavation of the overgrown dyke system. The violet appeared on many areas of newly disturbed and excavated peat. Other seedlings were recorded when dense scrub thicket was cleared, exposing unvegetated ground, and also around the sites of brushwood fires, and on the edge of depressions made by pulling out sallow bushes. In some areas where scrub thicket was tall and dense, seed must have been lying dormant under this growth for thirty to forty years. The natural habitat of this plant in the undrained fens was probably an open vegetation of sedges and low-growing plants on a moist, relatively acid peat. After the draining of Whittlesey Mere, extensive peat cutting for fifty to sixty years would have preserved the open moist conditions which it likes, in spite of the exploitation of the original peat surface and the elimination of other plants unable to adapt to continual disturbance. In the more unfavourable environmental conditions of today, the fen violet depends on continued human intervention for its survival.

In Breckland a very fine study has been made by A. S. Watt[64] of the history and ecology of a number of rare plants of open ground conditions. There is evidence that some of these may have reached this country through the agency of neolithic man, who first cultivated the Breckland soils. Other species, such as the ground pine (*Ajuga chamaepytis*), glabrous rupture-wort (*Herniaria glabra*), grape hyacinth (*Muscari atlanticum*), and star-of-Bethlehem (*Ornithogalum umbellatum*), are all weeds of Rhenish vineyards and may have been introduced to England with the vine. Watt distinguishes three groups of rarities, graded according to their competitive power and requiring different types of management. In Group 1 *Carex ericetorum,* sickle medick (*Medicago falcata*), and Böhmer's cat's-tail (*Phleum phleoides*) are species able to survive in the closest sward of ungrazed chalky pasture, dominated by the relatively low-growing grasses *Festuca ovina, Helictotrichon pratense,* and *Koeleria cristata.* Group 2 consists of perennials such as the Spanish catchfly (*Silene otites*), spiked speedwell (*Veronica spicata* ssp. *spicata*), and field southernwood (*Artemisia campestris*), which can become established on bare ground or in the short turf but are susceptible to rabbit grazing. In this case, competing species may have to be controlled by light or periodic grazing which should be discontinued before the plants flower, so that seed can form and be shed without disturbance and damage. Group 3 is the largest and consists of nine annuals and two small perennials. They are all characterized by low competitive power and require very open conditions. Wild thyme (*Thymus serpylifolium*) and spring speedwell (*Veronica verna*) hold their own in short turf which is heavily grazed by rabbits, while wall bedstraw (*Galium parisiense*) is a natural component of highly calcareous dry soils, occurring in abandoned chalk pits, so that the recreation of suitable habitats by excavation should be possible. The grass *Apera interrupta,* and the speedwells *Veronica praecox* and *Veronica triphyllos,* are closely restricted to arable and fallow soils and might be best preserved on arable reserves which are periodically ploughed or harrowed, but without the use of fertilizers and herbicides. *Crassula tillaea* grows well on the soil of pathways which have been consolidated by light trampling.

On chalk grasslands in Kent, an unusual reason was discovered for the scarcity of the monkey orchid (*Orchis simia*) apart from the usual threats from rabbit grazing and plant collectors. In this case very little fertile seed was set. Fertilization is normally accomplished by insect visitors to the flowers, which accidentally transfer the pollinia to the surface of the stigmata. H. M. Wilks found that this process could easily be done by hand using a broken grass stem, and plants fertilized in this way were soon producing quantities of fertile seed which he collected and sowed in suitable areas adjacent to the colony[65]. From the one plant he found in 1955, the colony grew to 256 plants in 1966. Artificial management of this type is disapproved of by some naturalists, who think it is too great an interference with natural processes. However, in cases of extreme rarity where local extinction may occur, temporary drastic remedies are sometimes necessary to strengthen or re-establish a viable population.

Lepidoptera and other invertebrates

Many species of attractive butterflies and moths are comparatively easy to rear, and this may be the reason why entomologists have been so enthusiastic about introducing or re-introducing them in many parts of the country. Most of these attempts have been unsuccessful or else go unrecorded, so that the long-term results are not known. However, the ability to rear large numbers of certain rare insects in captivity is a

Figure 37. Large blue butterfly. An endangered species now confined to a very few sites in the south-west.

potentially valuable technique for re-establishing a population or strengthening an existing one. This approach has been used successfully to increase the population of the purple emperor butterfly on a woodland site in the Midlands, and has been of particular value in the case of the large copper butterfly (pages 106-110) thanks to the expert management of a captive population by H. G. Short. At Wicken Fen, similar attempts have been made to re-introduce the swallowtail butterfly, but so far without success. The black and brown hairstreak butterflies have also been studied in recent years from a conservation viewpoint. Both feed on the common blackthorn *Prunus spinosa*. The former lay their eggs on twigs with flower buds high up on old blackthorn bushes along the rides, clearings and edges of woodlands. Brown hairstreaks prefer younger blackthorn, particularly around the margins of woodlands and in hedgerows. J. A. Thomas found that hedgerows were an important habitat for the brown hairstreak but that, because most ova are laid on the projecting young shoots, about 80 per cent are lost when the hedge is trimmed[66]. Hedgerow management may therefore be an important factor in the survival of local colonies. The large blue butterfly is probably the rarest native British species and is confined to a very few sites in the south-west. Its larvae first feed on wild thyme but are later taken by certain species of ants into their nests where they feed on ant larvae. This butterfly has proved very difficult to rear in captivity so, at present, the best hope for survival is protection of the surviving colonies.

Dragonflies are a group which can be encouraged by comparatively simple conservation techniques. Many species are territorial and able to breed in water bodies of small size, such as ponds and dykes, depending on depth and movement of water, and whether it is alkaline or acid. These habitats can be created fairly easily on nature reserves and are a good way of establishing the more common species.

The large copper butterfly

This very beautiful butterfly is probably the best known of insect re-introductions in this country, and since 1960 its ecology and management have been studied fairly closely[67]. The native race *Lycaena dispar dispar* was formerly well established in the Huntingdonshire fens but became very scarce in the 1840s due, it is said, to over-collecting.

Figure 38. Large copper butterfly (female). Bred at Woodwalton, on great water dock leaf.

The last specimen recorded was taken in 1851, at the time of the drainage and reclamation of the Whittesley Mere area, its traditional breeding site. In 1927 the almost identical Dutch race *Lycaena dispar batavus* was successfully established on Woodwalton Fen and three years later on Wicken Fen. In 1942 it disappeared from the latter reserve when the Adventurers Fen area was reclaimed for agriculture.

L. d. batavus is normally single-brooded in Britain, laying its eggs on the great water dock (*Rumex hydrolapathum*)—its only foodplant—in late summer. The eggs hatch after a week or so and the larvae feed for about three weeks before moving down to the base of the plant to overwinter in the litter, especially the dead dock leaves of the previous year. They emerge in the spring to continue feeding and finally pupate some time in June. About thirty days later the imagines appear. The population at Woodwalton Fen has been counted each year since 1960 and has seldom exceeded a total of about 350 adult insects. In some years it has been much lower, but after 1968, when extinction was caused by a summer flood, large numbers of larvae and pupae from captive stock were used for re-establishment.

The population is at risk at several points in the annual life cycle. Mortality is greatest (about 95 per cent) in the early stages, from oviposition to hibernation. Counts of hibernating larvae in mid-winter have been almost exactly the same as for larvae emerging in the spring, so losses during diapause are probably minimal. There is a further 75 per cent loss from spring emergence to pupation, so that if less than 100 larvae survive the winter, as has frequently been the case, the number of imagines would be too low to ensure an adequate number of eggs for the next generation. Consequently the practice, since 1927, of collecting larvae in the spring for rearing in the protection of muslin-covered cages has ensured the survival of the insect. Without this protection only about 15 per cent of the spring larvae would reach pupation. Until recently it was thought that these losses were due to parasitism by the tachinid fly *Phryxe vulgaris,* but experiments with larvae in cages of different mesh size have shown that mortality due to birds and small mammals during the summer months was six times as great as that due to invertebrate predators and parasites.

As might be expected with a marsh insect, the hibernating larvae can tolerate long periods of submergence, provided they have entered diapause. However, early flooding in the autumn will delay or prevent the downward movement from the leaves to the ground litter. Experiments with 484 larvae on flooded and unflooded plants showed that 22 per cent succeeded in penetrating the water barrier while 78 per cent hibernated on the upper parts of the plants. Under natural conditions, the above-ground hibernating larvae might be expected to be more vulnerable to predation by birds, and even to drift away on flood water when the dead plant stems break off. Severe flooding in the summer months is rare but the actively feeding larvae would be drowned or, as happened in July 1968, the worst summer flood since August 1912, the newly emerged females found that most of the dock plants were submerged in deep water and not available for oviposition.

Although mortality of larvae can be reduced at critical stages in the life cycle, a more difficult management problem is the manipulation of the fen environment to ensure adequate numbers of the foodplant. There are two main difficulties: the seed of the great water dock requires relatively open conditions on waterlogged peat for successful germination but this type of habitat (Elton's Aquatic/Terrestrial Transition—Open Ground Zone) disappeared from the Fen as the water table fell, and succession led to the spread of taller herbs and bush growth. This problem was eventually overcome by removing the woody growth and excavating a series of shallow depressions with gently sloping sides. Dock seed, which was shed and dispersed through the winter, drifted on to the exposed margins and germinated as the water table began to fall in the spring. However, it is known that female large coppers are often selective when searching for food plants for egg-laying. Docks growing by the edge of water are avoided, as are large plants with an abundance of leaves. The preferred plant seems to be of medium size, two to three feet (0.5-1 m) in height, with five to seven leaves, growing away from water in vegetation of about the same height. But such plants occur in conditions which are not favourable for germination. The management programme therefore had to include a regime of rotational peat excavations to create optimum conditions for the food plant but allowing succession to take place so that after a few years the docks were growing in a continuous vegetation cover.

These requirements have been successfully met in Compartments 93 and 94 (Figure 39), which are isolated by thick bush growth from the traditional large copper breeding area to the north. However, as succession took place and tall herbs spread over the peat cuttings, it was found that in spite of the presence of large numbers of dock plants, very few eggs were laid. It seemed likely that the tall fen herbs and reeds were smothering those dock plants of optimum size and perhaps making them inaccessible to the females. Three management treatments were applied

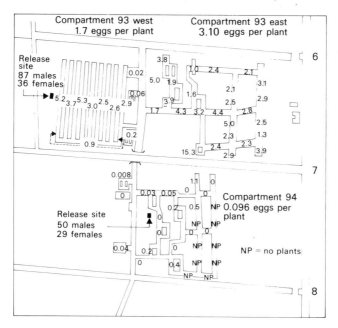

Figure 39. The distribution of eggs of the large copper butterfly in Compartments 93 and 94 in relation to number of adult insects, points of release, and condition of vegetation.

in 1972 to test this hypothesis. Compartment 93 West was mown early in the year. Compartment 93 East was grazed by six Galloway bullocks for eight weeks in May and June, and Compartment 94 was left undisturbed. In early July, when egg-laying began, the vegetation height in 93 West reached about 4 ft (1-1.5 m), but with a thick growth of reed 5-6 feet (1.5-2 m) on the eastern and southern sides, in 93 East vegetation height averaged 2-3 ft (0.5-1 m) but with local patches of taller herbs, and in 94 there was a fairly uniform growth of dense reed and herbs reaching 5-6 feet. The numbers and sites of release of the imagines together with the resulting distribution of eggs are shown in Figure 39.

Although furthest from the points of release, the highest mean number of eggs per plant was recorded in Compartment 93 East, where the docks were more exposed: twenty-eight times greater than the mean number of eggs per plant in Compartment 94, where most of the docks were smothered. Compartment 93 West, which has an overall mean value between these figures, was divided into seven blocks lying at increasing distances from the point of release. The mean number of eggs per plant calculated from each block showed a steady fall with increasing distance, and much lower values were recorded for the reed-dominated sections on the east and south sides. In other parts of the Fen it has been shown that, even where the habitat appears to be uniformly favourable, the largest number of eggs tends to be laid nearest to the point of release.

The example of the large copper shows that management for a single species of high conservation value and popular appeal may be complicated and difficult. The habitat has become less favourable as natural succession progresses, the water table has fallen steadily, and the breeding area needs regular maintenance both for the germination of the food plant and the requirements of the insect, while the total area available is probably too small for the population to build up to a safe level. These factors, together with the isolation of the Fen and absence of the insect elsewhere, make the species particularly vulnerable to extinction. Nevertheless its preservation is worthwhile, for it attracts many visitors to the reserve each year, it is an ideal subject for studies in ecological management, and it is also of scientific interest because it is claimed that after forty-two years of isolation the stock has a colour pattern slightly different from the extinct *L. d. dispar* and the Dutch *L. d. batavus*[68]. In addition, the status of the native population in the Dutch fens is becoming more precarious.

The raft spider

Insects have a monopoly of beautiful species which attract a good deal of attention from the public; most other arthropods are treated with suspicion or dislike. Much of this attitude is based on ignorance or superstition, as for instance, in the case of spiders. *Dolomedes plantarius* is one of the most striking British spiders, not only because of its large size, but for the beautiful colouring of orange stripes on the brown cephalothorax. It lives by the water's edge and is known from only one locality in Britain, unlike its close relative *Dolomedes fimbriatus,* which is fairly widespread. The single British locality is a fen nature reserve on the borders of Norfolk and Suffolk, formerly an important source of peat for the homes of the poor in nearby villages[69]. Unlike other areas, where peat turves were cut from long trenches, the practice here was to dig circular depressions some two to three yards (2-3 m) in diameter and half to one yard (0.5-1 m) depth. Around each was a hard uncut pathway used to stack the turves and transport them out of the Fen. The pits are now overgrown or waterfilled, and provide an excellent habitat for *Dolomedes plantarius.*

The common name of this species describes its habit of resting motionless on the surface of the water, waiting for flying or aquatic insects to come within reach. When alarmed the spider runs down the stem of an aquatic plant and remains submerged until the danger is passed. In July and August the splendid female, large enough to span the palm of one's hand, spins an open (brood) web in the fen vegetation up to two feet above the water surface, where the egg sac is taken when ready to hatch. The young disperse among the web strands and eventually move away into the fen vegetation where they live until reaching maturity at about two years old. While still less than half grown, the young spiders may spend much of their time away from the water and are even found on the foliage of bushes and low trees. However, adult males and females do not seem to wander far from the water surface, probably because, when they reach full size, the water provides a means of retreating quickly to safety. A spider as large as this could not easily hide or move rapidly enough in dense vegetation to avoid predators such as mice and shrews.

The pools of water are therefore essential to the survival of this rare and interesting species but the fen water table has fallen in recent years due to drainage works. Management now requires the re-excavation of existing pools and the digging of new ones in places where the water table fluctuations are least. In the absence of natural pools and peat cuttings, both of which sustained the species in the past, artificial methods are required if its specialized habitat conditions are to be met.

Introductions to nature reserves

Animals and plants have been introduced into this country accidentally or deliberately, by the agency of man, from at least neolithic times. The rabbit is said to have been brought here by the Normans in the eleventh century, the sycamore in the fifteenth or sixteenth century, and the rate of accidental introduction through commerce, roads, railways and canals speeded up rapidly in the nineteenth and twentieth centuries. The countryside, including nature reserves, has been greatly influenced by some of the more successful introduced animals, notably the American grey squirrel (introduced in 1876 and subsequent years), the coypu (introduced from South America in 1930 for fur farms, some escaping soon after), and the American mink (introduced for fur farms in 1929, although the first feral breeding record was not until 1956). The coypu caused considerable damage to the plant communities of nature reserves in the Norfolk Broads, particularly during the 1940s and 1950s before the severe winter of 1962. More recently the Chinese water deer (introduced to Woburn Abbey in 1900) has established a breeding population on Woodwalton Fen NNR, where it eats down the first leaves of the great water dock in the spring, so that some plants are not able to recover in time to provide food for the emerging larvae of the large copper butterfly.

Such problems are questions of eradication or control, but in other circumstances it is sometimes desirable, for scientific and other reasons, to introduce or re-introduce a particular species, or even a wildlife community, to a nature reserve. Examples of situations which may make this necessary are as follows:

1. A rare species may have disappeared from a particular area because of over-collecting, temporary habitat change, or an unusual combination of natural circumstances. Although it may occur elsewhere, re-introduction is considered necessary because of its general scarcity. Examples are the rare annual plants mentioned for Breckland.
2. A species becomes extinct on its only known British station but very similar stock is available from a foreign country. The large copper butterfly is one example and other species may reach this stage in the future, for instance the large blue butterfly.
3. A species believed extinct in this country is re-discovered but at a new site, and it is thought advisable to establish additional colonies.
4. It is desirable to create new habitats. It may be necessary to plant trees to extend an existing woodland site or to underplant where there is no regeneration. Aquatic animals and plants may be introduced to a newly excavated pond. Where the site is completely artificial (a worked-out gravel pit, for instance), extensive landscaping and planting may be necessary to create a desired range of habitats.

There is often a strong feeling among ecologists against introductions of any kind, although some *re*-introductions are acceptable. This is understandable because of the many occasions in the past when introductions, whether intentional or not, have resulted in species becoming pests (e.g. the coypu). We are also aware that the indigenous faunas and floras of some other countries, and particularly oceanic islands, have suffered serious losses because of unwise introductions.

Moreover, there is a conviction that wildlife communities should be allowed to gain or lose species in relation to changing environmental factors without interference by man. This, it is argued, is a natural process which should be preserved partly for scientific interest and partly to avoid more artificiality entering the system. Most biologists would agree that this would be a strong argument in a country which had not felt the impact of industrialization, modern technology, and a high population density. However Britain has all these things, and landscape changes which affect wildlife may take place rapidly and often on a grand scale. Modern man has accelerated the rate of extinction and caused even more species to enter the ranks of 'rare' and 'very rare'. Technological progress and urbanization undoubtedly continue and, as semi-natural habitats and sites of rare species are swept away or reduced, the need to recreate or re-establish them elsewhere will increase. Extinction is final, and both scientific knowledge and our cultural heritage are diminished by it.

Safeguards against the abuse of introductions of plants and animals have been discussed by the Society for the Promotion of Nature Reserves and a number of suggestions have been made[70]. These have been incorporated in the following proposals relating to examples 1 to 4 on page 112.

(*a*) Individuals for re-introduction should be taken from populations in the same part of the geographical range as the reserve so that the new stock resembles the old as closely as possible. The habitat and other environmental factors should be such that the re-introduction has every chance of success. This is particularly important in the case of example 3, otherwise valuable stock would be wasted.

(*b*) Introductions using foreign stock of species now extinct in Britain would be valid only in exceptional circumstances, for example, if the status of the species concerned was threatened in Europe and there were the strongest scientific reasons for believing that it could re-establish successfully on a nature reserve in this country. This was not the case in 1927 when Dutch stock of the large copper butterfly was introduced into Woodwalton Fen, but since then there has been a contraction of suitable breeding sites in its native locality and in a European sense the insect may soon be an endangered sub-species.

(*c*) Alien species should not be introduced to nature reserves. Because they have never been part of a wildlife community in this country, their behaviour is likely to be unpredictable and they might increase rapidly at the expense of native species. Alien trees, shrubs, and plants usually have poor faunas because the indigenous animals of this country are not adapted to them. Consequently they add little to the biological diversity of nature reserves.

(*d*) If introductions are thought necessary for the rapid creation of a new landscape or an extension of an existing reserve on previously exploited land, they should be planned on the basis of reproducing the plant and animal communities characteristic of that region. In other words, one asks the question: 'Which native species would be most likely to colonize this area in the absence of man?'

(*e*) Finally, and of great importance, all introductions should be fully recorded and documented, the Biological Records Centre at Monks Wood Experimental Station acting as a national data bank for this type of information.

Conservation and collecting

Two of the outstanding characteristics of human nature are curiosity and possessiveness. Man has no doubt responded to these by collecting living and inanimate objects of nature over a long period, and it should come as no surprise that the practice was highly developed before ecology became a science. The fashion of amassing glass cases of stuffed birds and cabinets of eggs and butterflies has now largely disappeared from this country, partly through legislation and partly through education and a change in public opinion. However, the number of naturalists and biologists has continued to increase and it is more important than ever that they have adequate material for research, education, and leisure activities. Field studies, photography, filming, recording, and listing have all developed as new interests which substitute for the collecting enthusiasm of the last century.

Nevertheless the popular interest in collecting is still strong and, provided it is properly controlled and directed, it still has an important function. Many young people attracted to wildlife studies like to be able to handle and possess the things that interest them and, if properly supervised by conservation-conscious teachers, collecting is a useful educational tool. Indeed most biologists, amateur or professional, will confess to starting their interest by collecting common plants or insects. Some adults never progress beyond the acquisitive urge to build up a natural history collection, but if this is practised selfishly, damage may well be done. Inevitably rare species are most sought after and, in the case of an insect occupying a specialized habitat, the latter may be destroyed in the search, as well as the specimen taken; for example, by the total destruction of a rotten log, the removal of all the bark from a dead tree, or simply by leaving stones overturned instead of repositioning them when searching for a rare ground-living animal.

Sometimes, light traps are also criticised as another form of destructive collecting. Large catches may be taken and killed although very few specimens are kept. Many entomologists believe that this has no influence on insect populations but, because others feel concern, the Nature Conservancy only permits the use, on National Nature Reserves, of light traps which allow unwanted specimens to be released.

Inevitably there is some inconsistency in the attitudes and policies to collecting. Popular groups such as birds are well supported by public opinion so that now there is effective legislation to protect all but pest species. Other animals (apart from game), and all plants, are only protected on areas which have byelaws to this effect. Some rare or endangered insects and certain native mammals should certainly be protected wherever they occur, but the need is perhaps greatest for an increasing number of plants. Some very scarce species are beautiful and conspicuous, and unlike animals, cannot escape the collector or gardener by running or flying.

The scientist engaged on taxonomic, genetical, or biological studies often needs to take live material for his research. However, the selfish scientist can do as much harm as a selfish collector and the comment 'but I'm doing research' is no excuse for behaviour which would not be tolerated in others. Collecting on National Nature Reserves, for whatever purpose, is allowed only by permit. However, this is not meant to discourage those with a genuine interest, in the knowledge that we are dealing with a renewable resource which can usually sustain some cropping without populations being endangered. It is also a valuable means of adding to the knowledge of the reserve's wildlife. This approach could perhaps be the basis of a more comprehensive policy on collecting throughout the country—we should *tolerate* the ethics, *regulate* the practice, and *educate* the collector.

7
Conservation Research and the Future

Today there are almost as many prophets as prophecies about the condition of our environment at the beginning of the next millenium, but, whether optimists or pessimists, we do not need a crystal ball to predict some of the more difficult problems which the next generation of wildlife conservationists will have to solve. Some trends are already clear and perhaps we should already be considering a wildlife counterpart of the 'Blueprint for survival'[71] recently proposed for human populations. The 'final' total of National Nature Reserves in Britain is not yet known but may be in the region of 250-300, to which one should add some 7-800 lower category areas owned or administered by other bodies. The selection and establishment of nature reserves, the regulation of access, and the specialized estate work which is needed still present considerable problems, but the necessary expertise based on twenty years' experience is largely available. On the other hand the ecological knowledge required for the successful scientific management of wildlife communities and species is still rudimentary and research must not be allowed to lag behind the growing needs of the future.

Wildlife in an urban society

We estimate (see Appendix, page 124) that roughly 10 per cent of the land surface is providing some protection for our fauna and flora, although only one-eleventh of this total is within the present series of 135 NNRs. The very comprehensive *Conservation Review*, recently completed by the Nature Conservancy, of all the major natural formations in Britain and the extent to which they occur on National Nature Reserves, has clearly indicated the deficiencies. Some of these will be made good, but the rate of increase in the number and the total area of reserves has been low for some years and, with land values at their present level, further substantial progress will demand very considerable resources.

Meanwhile urban expansion, road building, and industrial developments of many kinds, are themselves making much higher demands on the available land. At the same time agriculture is becoming more specialized and dependent on machines, artificial fertilizers, and biocides to maintain its $3\frac{1}{2}$ per cent annual growth in production. In lowland Britain, where these trends are most evident, housing estates and the spread of suburbia are already creeping up to the margins of some nature reserves. This, together with man-made forests and intensive agriculture, will accentuate the problems of isolation referred to in Chapter 4.

Expanding populations and dwindling areas of open land will result in increasing public use of many reserves in open and attractive landscapes. The impact of human activities is now being studied by a number of ecologists, particularly the effects of disturbance, trampling, and terrestrial eutrophication. However, all reserves are used to some extent by people, whether by a few specialists or by large numbers of the general public. The influence these activities have on wildlife is as important an aspect of management as any other deserving study. Not all these effects are detrimental, as can be seen at Wicken Fen and in Breckland, where light trampling preserves open conditions required by certain low-growing plants.

One of the most rapid developments in the creation of countryside amenity areas for the public is the establishment of Country Parks by local authorities and some private individuals, in conjunction with the Countryside Commission, which can make grants for up to 75 per cent of the costs. Of the 94 already in existence, about 20 per cent include sites or parts of sites scheduled for their wildlife interest (SSSI). This places a special responsibility on those who manage the Parks and on the Countryside Commission which advises them. Although the provision of outdoor amenities is the main function of these areas, they present an excellent opportunity for co-operation between sociologists (to study the distribution, activities, and numbers of people) and ecologists (to measure the biological effects on different types of habitats and their wildlife). This type of information will be relevant not only to management problems on the more popular nature reserves but also in National Parks, Forest Parks, and to the large areas of countryside owned by the National Trust.

Some Country Parks include land previously cultivated, and management includes the problem of restoring a type of vegetation attractive to the public. New swards of hard-wearing grasses can easily be grown, but in some cases, as on the chalk, a more attractive type, comparable to semi-natural grassland, would be preferred. A species-rich sward would normally take many years to develop, but current research on seed viability, soil conditions, and competitive relationships between species may soon find a way to recreate such grasslands in a comparatively short time. This information would also be valuable for reserve management, the maintenance of some historical monuments such as earthworks, and the restoration of land where the vegetation has been destroyed by intensive public use.

These examples of research in conservation ecology emphasize an essential feature which is often forgotten, that is, its interdependence with other disciplines. Conservation cannot become an accepted form of land use unless those who practise it work with sociologists and planners. And conversely, these professions are learning that the reliability of their decisions concerning the land depends on adequate ecological knowledge. Fortunately there is reason for optimism now that ecologists are being employed in planning offices and in industry, but the research on which competent advice must be based still needs further support.

Nationalism in conservation is not enough

Wildlife does not recognize political boundaries, and with very few exceptions the species of plants and animals in Britain have for long also been Europeans. Most of our breeding birds winter in countries further south and others come here from northern breeding territories. International bird preservation has perhaps made more progress than other groups, although protection north of the Alps does not prevent some birds being caught and eaten as they migrate south through Europe. Project MAR is an international effort to protect European wetland areas which are important feeding stations for marsh and aquatic birds on migration routes. Although progress to protect these areas is slow, international research projects have been developed to improve knowledge on the numbers, movement and feeding requirements of wetland birds.

European countries are also establishing additional National Parks and particularly the more numerous Regional, or, as they are sometimes called, Nature Parks. Already there are important Parks which lie across

Figure 40. View of former agricultural land in a Danish Nature Park. Comparable to British Country Park.

international frontiers, for example between France and Spain in the Pyrenées, Germany and Belgium, Switzerland and Italy, and Poland and Czechoslovakia. Joint consultations on management take place and more parks of this type are planned for the future. Britain's contribution to the organizational aspect of international conservation affairs, particularly in bird protection, to the work of the International Union for the Conservation of Nature and Natural Resources, and the Council for Europe, has been very significant. Lately it has given strong support to Flora Europea, a highly organized plan to publish a modern study of the plants in Europe, including their distribution. This will be of great value for conservation planning. In addition a network of study groups is being organized to map the distribution of European invertebrates, with the object of publishing a series of maps similar to, but on a smaller scale than, the Atlas of the British Flora. Recording basic information of this type is an essential first step in biological survey and much has already been achieved in Britain by the Biological Records Centre at the Monks Wood Experimental Station.

Although conservation is attracting increasing support in continental countries, none has yet conducted a scientific survey comparable to the comprehensive assessment made in the Nature Conservancy's Conservation Review. Moreover, because the emphasis in the majority of countries is on the recreational function of National Parks and similar areas, most have been established in mountainous and hilly regions because the public prefers wild landscapes and grand scenery. Unfortunately this bias in the representation of habitats on protected areas has not been balanced by the creation of an adequate number of nature reserves in lowland districts. The preoccupation of some European countries with planning studies, population surveys, and the financial resources required for more amenity areas, seems to have turned attention away from the ecological work which will be needed to ensure that these semi-natural landscapes survive unspoilt.

During the last twenty-three years Britain has made significant progress in developing a scientific approach to conservation and nature reserve management. Much of this work is almost unknown in the greater part of Europe, although the Netherlands and Sweden are engaged on similar Government-supported research. Nevertheless ecology as a subject is attracting increasing interest in many institutes and universities. Political and economic association with the European Community could stimulate much closer co-operation between conservation scientists, perhaps with as much success as that achieved by the International Biological Programme. We all share the same problems of highly-developed, over-populated countries, and Britain's greater experience in conservation work could help others to avoid our mistakes. On the other hand, the opportunity to see, in a European context, our own work on ecological survey and distribution, on plant and animal communities, species studies, and nature reserve management could add immeasurably to its interest and its overall value.

Appendix: The Development of the Conservation Movement

It has been said that the first conservationist in Britain was Saint Cuthbert, who protected the wildfowl on the Farne Islands 1300 years ago. Several hundreds of years later the Norman Kings unknowingly made their own contribution by establishing royal hunting forests where all the larger wild animals, particularly deer, were preserved for sport. The most famous to survive to the present day is the New Forest of Hampshire: 66 000 acres (27 500 ha) of woodland, heath, and bog which now form one of the richest wildlife regions in Britain. In addition much of the area is open to the public, attracting over $3\frac{1}{2}$ million visitors a year[72]. Another ancient royal hunting preserve is Epping Forest on the north side of London. It is now managed by the Corporation of the City of London and includes 4000 acres (1666 ha) of woodland and 2000 acres (833 ha) of grazing land, nearly all open to the visitor. The biological interest of these areas is exceptional because of the diverse vegetation cover, and hence a good deal of the animal life has survived destruction for many centuries.

A positive approach to conserving wildlife in Britain was comparatively late in developing and probably began with the creation of three important voluntary organizations. These are the Royal Society for the Protection of Birds (founded in 1889), the National Trust (founded in 1895), and the Society for the Promotion of Nature Reserves (founded in 1912).

Some of the earliest nature reserves in Britain were fenland areas. Between 1890 and 1900 small parts of Wicken Fen near Cambridge were bought by entomologists and botanists. These pieces of fen were later presented to the National Trust and by 1923 had reached a total of 521 acres (217 ha). The first part of Woodwalton Fen, Huntingdonshire, was purchased in 1910 and presented to the Society for the Promotion of Nature Reserves. The benefactor was the Hon. N. C. Rothschild, who, in 1915, made the first national survey of areas of outstanding wildlife interest which in his opinion deserved protection. However, public and government support was insufficient and between the wars progress was maintained only by the action of a few far-sighted individuals who achieved much by determination and enthusiasm.

One of those deserving special mention is Dr Sidney Long, who founded the Norfolk Naturalists' Trust, the first of its kind, in 1926. In 1912 Long had assisted Professor F. W. Oliver in raising a fund to purchase Blakeney Point, which is now one of the best-known National Trust properties. Scolt Head Island, a dune ridge four miles (6.4 km) long, also off the Norfolk coast, had a special attraction for Long because it was quite unspoilt. In 1923 he organized a public appeal and succeeded in buying the greater part of the island, which was also presented to the National Trust. In 1954 it was leased to the Nature Conservancy and became a National Nature Reserve. Long's object in forming a Trust was to create a local organization with a constitution which enabled it to own and manage land for wildlife conservation. By 1949, when the Nature Conservancy was formed, Norfolk had a fine series of reserves quite unrivalled by any other British county. No other County Naturalists' Trust was formed until 1945, when a second was established in Yorkshire.

During the war years, however, many discussions had been organized by distinguished biologists who were concerned about the disappearance of wildlife habitats. There was a growing conviction that an overall national plan was needed and that it could only succeed if it had government backing. The initiative was taken by the Society for the Promotion of Nature Reserves. A Nature Reserves Investigation Committee (NRIC) was formed and prepared a series of Memoranda dealing with the selection, acquisition, and management of sites which might be suitable as nature reserves. Two valuable reports describing the range of vegetation types which should be preserved on national nature reserves were published by the British Ecological Society, whose influence was to become a decisive factor when final plans were presented to the Government.

In 1943 the SPNR organized a series of regional sub-committees who were asked to prepare, for the NRIC, lists of sites for each county in England and Wales. They were also asked to say which were of sufficient importance to be made into 'National Reserves'. At the same time the British Ecological Society, the Royal Society for the Protection of Birds and the Royal Entomological Society prepared their own lists for the central Committee.

The basic data were now available and in 1945 the Government appointed the first official body, the Wildlife Conservation Special Committee. This Committee included Sir (then Dr) Julian Huxley, FRS, as Chairman, later succeeded by Sir (then Professor) A. G. Tansley, FRS, and Captain C. Diver and Mr E. M. Nicholson: the last two were to become the first and second Director-Generals, respectively, of the Nature Conservancy. The Special Committee's report to Parliament, published in July 1947[1], included a wide range of proposals dealing with nature conservation and ecological research, most of which were accepted by the Government and written into the National Parks and Access to the Countryside Act of 1949. Out of this was formed the Nature Conservancy.

The work of the regional sub-committees of NRIC stimulated a number of local societies to think hard about their own interests in conservation work, and in 1948 the third Naturalists' Trust was formed in Lincolnshire. The remarkable success and influence of this Trust were undoubtedly responsible for the creation of others, and in 1959 eight were active in different counties. In 1971 the total had grown to thirty-nine, covering all parts of England, Wales, and Scotland, and the membership had risen from 2700 in 1960 to 80 000 in 1973.

The potential value of County Trusts was not realized in 1947 and it may have been thought that the existence of a national body would make local initiative unnecessary. Today the two-tiered structure of the organization of conservation in Britain is accepted without question as essential to the success of the movement. The Nature Conservancy takes the main responsibility for the National Nature Reserves and other national problems, while the voluntary bodies select and manage a network of smaller sites. The 1949 Act also includes powers to enable local authorities to establish Local Nature Reserves, of which there are now thirty-one.

The 1947 Report of the Wildlife Conservation Special Committee (Cmd 7122) proposed a 'Biological Service' which would be responsible for the establishment and management of nature reserves and the provision of advice on conservation. The necessary research and survey was to be conducted by mobile specialists working on the major types of habitats on nature reserves. In addition to the Biological Service, the Report recommended the establishment of terrestrial research institutes to develop ecological studies. Two were formed in the early years of the Conservancy, one at Grange-over-Sands on the south side of the Lake District, and a second near Wareham in the delightful heath country of Dorset.

A regional organization was established by the Nature Conservancy in 1952, and there are now six regions in England, two in Wales and three in Scotland, the scientific staff being responsible for managing NNRs, selection and establishment of Sites of Special Scientific Interest, and liaison with local authorities, government departments, and voluntary bodies. Their duties increased so rapidly that less time became available for reserve management studies, and Habitat Teams of scientific staff were formed to help with this work. In 1963 a new Experimental Station, adjacent to the Monks Wood NNR in Huntingdonshire, was opened. It is now the largest of the Conservancy's research stations and includes staff working on scientific methods of conservation, biological survey, wildlife management, and the effects of pesticides on wildlife.

In addition to 135 NNRs, 700 Naturalists' Trust reserves, 31 Local Nature Reserves, 9 Forest Nature Reserves (made by agreement between the Forestry Commission and the Conservancy), 3165 Sites of Special Scientific Interest (SSSI), and 50 reserves of the Royal Society for the Protection of Birds, there are 10 National Parks, 94 Country Parks, 8 National Forest Parks, 21 National Wildfowl Refuges and the 400 000 acres (166 666 ha) owned by the National Trust. Much of the National Trust land is farmed, but public access is permitted over 200 000 acres (83 333 ha) of heaths, moors, mountains, coasts, and woodland. The last five categories of land are managed primarily for purposes other than the protection of wildlife, but nevertheless they preserve a wide range of habitats and make a most important contribution to conservation throughout the country. If we consider all the categories of protected land which have been mentioned, bearing in mind that there may be considerable overlap such as NNRs in National Parks and many SSSIs also being Naturalists' Trust reserves, we can make a very rough estimate that about 10 per cent of the total land surface of Britain is making some contribution to the protection of our fauna and flora.

Postscript

In August 1973 the Nature Conservancy Council Act was passed by Parliament. This Act created a new organization (responsible to the Department of the Environment) called the Nature Conservancy Council, made up of the administrative, management, and advisory sections of the former Nature Conservancy, which was a component body of the Natural Environment Research Council. The research institutes of the Nature Conservancy remain in the NERC and form part of the recently established Institute of Terrestrial Ecology.

Bibliography

1. MINISTRY OF TOWN AND COUNTRY PLANNING (1947). *Conservation of Nature in England and Wales,* report of the Wild Life Conservation Special Committee (England and Wales),Cmd 7122, London, H.M.S.O.
2. BROADS CONSORTIUM (1971). *Broadland Study and Plan,* report of the Broads Consortium Committee, Norwich, Norfolk County Council.
3. LOCKE, G. M. L. (1962). 'A sample survey of fields and other boundaries in Great Britain.' *Quarterly Journal of Forestry,* **56,** 137-144.
4. MOORE, N. W. (1968). 'The conservation of animals.' In: *Hedges and Hedgerow Trees,* edited by M. D. Hooper and M. W. Holdgate. Symposium No. 4, Monks Wood Experimental Station, The Nature Conservancy.
5. BENSON, G. B. C. and WILLIAMSON, K. (1972). 'Breeding birds of a mixed farm in Suffolk'. *Bird Study,* **19,** 34-50.
6. LAMBERT, J. M., JENNINGS, J. N., SMITH, C. T., GREEN, C. and HUTCHINSON, J. N. (1960). *The Making of the Broads,* Research Series No. 3, Royal Geographical Society.
7. CROMPTON, G. (1972). *History of Lakenheath Warren,* MS Report to the Nature Conservancy, London.
8. RACKHAM, O. (1971). 'Historical studies and woodland conservation.' In: *The Scientific Management of Animal and Plant Communities for Conservation,* edited by E. Duffey and A. S. Watt, British Ecological Society Symposium No. 11, Blackwell Scientific Publications, Oxford.
9. GRAYSON, A. J. and JONES, E. W. (1955). *Notes on the history of Wytham Estate,* Oxford, Imperial Forestry Institute.
10. ELTON, C. S. (1966). *The Pattern of Animal Communities,* London, Methuen.
11. PETERKEN, G. F. (1969). 'Development of vegetation in Staverton Park, Suffolk.' *Field Studies,* **3,** 1-39.
12. HOOPER, M. D. (1971). 'Hedges and local history.' In: *Hedges and Local History,* London, Standing Conference for Local History, for the National Council of Social Service.
13. BRADSHAW, A. D. (1971). 'The significance of hawthorns.' In: *Hedges and Local History,* Standing Conference for Local History, for the National Council of Social Service, London.
14. BOWEN, H. C. (1969). 'Archaeological fieldwork on settlements and land used in the later prehistoric and Roman period.' In: *Old Grassland—its Archaeological and Ecological Importance,* edited by J. Sheail and T. C. E. Wells, Symposium No. 5, Monks Wood Experimental Station, The Nature Conservancy.
15. WELLS, T. C. E. and BARLING, D. M. (1971). '*Pulsatilla vulgaris* Müll. Biological Flora No. 120.' *J. Ecology,* **59,** 275-292.

16. DUFFEY, E. (1972). 'Arachnological survey in relation to conservation.' *Proceedings of the 5th Arachnological Congress,* 105-17, Brno, Czechoslovak Academy of Sciences.
17. MOORE, N. W. (1962). 'The heaths of Dorset and their conservation.' *J. Ecology,* **50**, 369-391.
18. ELLIS, E. A. (1965). *The Broads,* London, Collins.
19. SUFFLING, E. R. (1887). *The Land of the Broads,* London.
20. VAN DER MAAREL, E. (1971). 'Plant species diversity in relation to management.' In: *The Scientific Management of Animal and Plant Communities for Conservation,* edited by E. Duffey and A. S. Watt, British Ecological Society Symposium No. 11, Blackwell Scientific Publications, Oxford.
21. SOUTHWOOD, T. R. E. (1966). *Ecological Methods, with particular reference to the study of insect populations,* London, Methuen.
22. PERRING, F. H. and WALTERS, S. M. (1962). *Atlas of the British Flora,* London, Nelson, for Botanical Society of the British Isles.
23. PERRING, F. H. (1970). 'The last seventy years.' In: *The Flora of a Changing Britain,* Botanical Society of the British Isles, Report No. 11.
24. HOOPER, M. D. (1971). 'The size and surroundings of nature reserves.' In: *The Scientific Management of Animal and Plant Communities for Conservation,* edited by E. Duffey and A. S. Watt, British Ecological Society Symposium No. 11, Blackwell Scientific Publications, Oxford.
25. TAMM, C. O. (1972). 'Survival and flowering of some perennial herbs. III. The behaviour of *Primula veris* on permanent plots.' *Oikos,* **23**, 159-166.
26. ØDUM, S. (1965). 'Germination of ancient seeds. Floristical observations and experiments with archaeologically dated soil samples.' *Dansk bot. Ark.,* **24**, 1-70.
27. FIELD, C. R. and LAWS, R. M. (1970). 'The distribution of the larger herbivores in the Queen Elizabeth National Park, Uganda.' *Journal of Applied Ecology,* **7**, 273-294.
28. DUFFEY, E. (1970). 'Habitat selection by spiders on saltmarsh in Gower.' *Nature in Wales,* **12**, 15-23.
29. MACFADYEN, A. (1963). *Animal Ecology. Aims and Methods,* 2nd edition, London, Pitman.
30. TANSLEY, A. G. (1949). *The British Isles and Their Vegetation,* Vol. 1, Cambridge, Cambridge University Press.
31. TRETZEL, E. (1955). 'Intragenerische Isolation und interspezifische Konkurrenz bei Spinnen.' *Z. Morph. u. Ökol. Tiere,* **44**, 43-162.
32. SOCIETY FOR THE PROMOTION OF NATURE RESERVES (1969). *Biological Sites Recording Scheme,* Society for the Promotion of Nature Reserves. Conservation Liaison Committee, Technical Publication No. 1.
33. SCHAEFFER, M. (1970). 'Einfluss der Raumstruktur in Landschaften der Meeresküste auf das Verteilungsmuster der Tierwelt.' *Zool. Jb. Syst.,* **97**, 55-124.
34. WELLS, T. C. E. (1972). In: *Monks Wood Experimental Station Report for 1969-71,* 48. The Nature Conservancy.
35. MORRIS, M. G. (1969). 'Differences between the invertebrate faunas of grazed and ungrazed chalk grassland. III. The heteropterous fauna.' *Journal of Applied Ecology,* **6**, 475-487.
36. MORRIS, M. G. (1971). 'The management of grassland for the conservation of invertebrate animals.' In: *The Scientific Management of Animal and Plant Communities for Conservation,* edited by E. Duffey and A. S. Watt, British Ecological Society Symposium No. 11, Blackwell Scientific Publications, Oxford.

37. DUFFEY, E. (1962). 'A population study of spiders in limestone grassland. Description of study area, sampling methods and population characteristics.' *Journal of Animal Ecology,* **31**, 571-599.
38. LENSINK, B. M. (1963). 'Distributional ecology of some Acrididae (Orthoptera) in the dunes of Voorne, Netherlands.' *Tijdschrift voor Entomologie,* **106**, 357-443.
39. VAN DER MAAREL, E. and LEERTOUWER, J. (1967). 'Variation in vegetation and species diversity along a local environmental gradient.' *Acta Bot. Neerl.,* **16**, 211-221.
40. DEN BOER, P. J. (1968). 'Spreading of risk and stabilization of animal numbers.' *Acta Biotheoretica,* **18**, 165-194.
41. WATT, A. S. (1947). 'Pattern and process in the plant community.' *Journal of Ecology,* **35**, 1-22.
42. DUFFEY, E. (1968). 'An ecological analysis of the spider fauna of sand dunes.' *Journal of Animal Ecology,* **37**, 641-674.
43. TISCHLER, W. (1963). 'Weitere Untersuchungen zur Ökologie der Schmalwanze *Ischnodemus sabuleti* Fall. (Hem., Lygaeidae).' *Zoologischer Anzeiger,* **171**, 339-349.
44. BRISTOWE, W. S. (1939). *The Comity of Spiders,* Vol. 1. London, Ray Society.
45. ARNOLD, G. A. and CROCKER, J. (1967). '*Arctosa perita* (Latr.) from colliery spoil heaps in Warwickshire and Leicestershire.' *British Spider Study Group Bulletin,* **35**, 7-8.
46. HEYDEMANN, B. (1960). 'Verlauf und Abhängigkeit von Spinnensukzessionen im Neuland der Nordseeküste'. *Verh. Deutsch. Zool. Ges. Bonn/Rhein,* 431-457.
47. DUFFEY, E. (1971). 'The management of Woodwalton Fen: a multidisciplinary approach.' In: *The Scientific Management of Animal and Plant Communities for Conservation,* edited by E. Duffey and A. S. Watt, Oxford, Blackwell Scientific Publications, British Ecological Society Symposium No. 11.
48. POORE, M. E. D. (1956). 'The ecology of Woodwalton Fen.' *Journal of Ecology,* **44**, 455-492.
49. LARSSON, T. (1972). *Distribution and Ornithological Aspects of Marshy Meadows in southern Sweden,* Royal College of Forestry, Research Notes No. 12. Stockholm.
50. ELLENBERG, H. and MUELLER-DOMBOIS, D. (1966). 'Tentative physiognomic-ecological classification of plant formations of the earth.' *Ber. geobot. Forsch. Inst. Rübel,* **37**, 21-55.
51. SHEAIL, J. (1971). *Rabbits and Their History,* Newton Abbot, David and Charles.
52. WELLS, T. C. E. (1973). *Chalk Grassland: Studies on its Conservation and Management,* edited by A. C. Jermy and P. A. Stott, Kent Trust for Nature Conservation.
53. WELLS, T. C. E. (1967). 'Changes in a population of *Spiranthes spiralis* (L.) Chevall, at Knocking Hoe National Nature Reserve, Bedfordshire, 1962-65.' *Journal of Ecology,* **55**, 83-99.
54. HARPER, J. L. and WHITE, J. (1971). 'The dynamics of plant populations.' *Proceedings of the Advanced Study Institute on Dynamics Numbers Populations (Oosterbeek, 1970),* 41-43.
55. WELLS, T. C. E. (1969). 'Botanical aspects of conservation management of chalk grasslands.' *Biological Conservation,* **2**, 36-44.
56. GREEN, B. H. (1972). 'The relevance of seral eutrophication and plant competition to the management of successional communities.' *Biological Conservation,* **4**, 378-384.

57. MORRIS, M. G. (1969). 'Populations of invertebrate animals and the management of chalk grassland in Britain.' *Biological Conservation*, 4, 225-231.
58. DUFFEY, E. (1963). 'Ecological studies on the spider fauna of the Malham Tarn area.' *Field Studies*, 1(5).
59. LUFF, M. L. (1966). 'The abundance and diversity of the beetle fauna of grass tussocks.' *Journal of Animal Ecology*, 35, 189-208.
60. WILLIAMSON, K. (1967). 'Some aspects of the scientific interest and management of scrub on nature reserves.' In: *The Biotic Effects of Public Pressures on the Environment*, edited by E. Duffey, Monks Wood Experimental Station Symposium No. 3, The Nature Conservancy.
61. SOUTHWOOD, T. R. E. (1960). 'The evolution of the insect-host tree relationship—a new approach.' *11th International Congress for Entomology, Vienna*, 651-655.
62. WARD, L. K. (1971). In: *Monks Wood Experimental Station Report for 1969-71*, 55-7, The Nature Conservancy.
63. DRING, M. J. and FROST, L. C. (1971). 'Studies of *Ranunculus ophioglossifolius* in relation to its conservation on the Badgeworth Nature Reserve, Gloucestershire, England.' *Biological Conservation*, 4, 48-56.
64. WATT, A. S. (1971). 'Rare species in Breckland: their management for survival.' *Journal of Applied Ecology*, 8, 593-609.
65. WILKS, H. M. (1966). 'The Monkey Orchid in Kent.' *Society for the Promotion of Nature Reserves Handbook, 1966.*
66. THOMAS, J. A. (1971), In: *Monks Wood Experimental Station Report for 1969-71*, 41-3, The Nature Conservancy.
67. DUFFEY, E. (1968). 'Ecological studies on the Large Copper butterfly *Lycaena dispar* Haw. *batavus* Obth. at Woodwalton Fen National Nature Reserve, Huntingdonshire.' *Journal of Applied Ecology*, 5, 69-96.
68. BINK, F. A. (1970). 'A review of the introductions of *Thersamonia dispar* Haw. (Lep., Lycaenidae) and the speciation problem.' *Entomologische Berichten*, 30, 179-183.
69. DUFFEY, E. (1958). '*Dolomedes plantarius.*' *Transactions of the Norfolk and Norwich Naturalists' Society*, 18, 1-5.
70. SOCIETY FOR THE PROMOTION OF NATURE RESERVES (1970). *A policy on Introductions to Nature Reserves*, Conservation Liaison Committee, Technical Publication No. 2
71. ANON. (1972). 'Blueprint for Survival.' *Ecologist*, 2(1), 2-42.
72. FORESTRY COMMISSION (1970). *Conservation of the New Forest*, a report for consultation prepared by officers drawn from the Forestry Commission, Hampshire County Council, the Nature Conservancy [and others].
73. CZAJKA, M. and BEDNARZ, S. (1972). 'Biology of *Pelecopsis bicapitata*, Miller 1938, Erigonidae.' *Proceedings of 5th Arachnological Congress*, 85-7, Brno, Czechoslovak Academy of Sciences.
74. SPARKS, B. W., WILLIAMS, R. B. G., and BELL, F. G. (1972). 'Presumed ground-ice depressions in East Anglia.' *Proc. R. Soc. Lond. A.*, 327, 329-43.

Index